THE HERALD DREAM

THE HERALD DREAM

An Approach to the
Initial Dream in Psychotherapy

Richard Kradin MD, IAAP

KARNAC

RC
489
.D74
K73
2006

First published in 2006 by
Karnac Books
118 Finchley Road, London NW3 5HT

Copyright © 2006 by Richard Kradin

The rights of Richard Kradin to be identified as the author of this work have been asserted in accordance with §§ 77 and 78 of the Copyright Design and Patents Act 1988.

British Library Cataloguing in Publication Data

A C.I.P. for this book is available from the British Library

ISBN10: 1-85575-450-9
ISBN13: 978-1-85575-450-8

Edited, designed, and typeset by RefineCatch Ltd, Bungay, Suffolk

Printed in Great Britain

www.karnacbooks.com

Dedication

This book is dedicated to parents who hoped that I would grow up to be a doctor but trained me to be an analyst; to Cheryl who taught me where the quotation marks go; to my kids who put up with a Jungian dad; and to Joe and Claude, who, respectively, are the best dog and cat in the world.

CONTENTS

LIST OF ILLUSTRATIONS

FOREWORD

I am privileged to teach a course on dream interpretation to trainees at the Center for Psychoanalytical Studies at the Massachusetts General Hospital. Whereas most of the trainees have been trained in modern psychoanalytical theory and technique, few are well acquainted with Jungian psychology or with its specific approach to dream interpretation. Jung suggested that the unconscious has *objective* qualities and that dreams can be accurately evaluated even in the absence of any *a priori* knowledge of the dreamer. It invariably comes as a surprise to trainees to discover how much information can be gleaned from dreams via such a symbolic approach.

My own Jungian training was preceded by years of psycho-analytic psychotherapeutic training during which I learned the importance of developmental history, oedipal dynamics, and of working in the transference. My interests in comparative religion and Buddhist psychology have also opened new avenues to my understanding of the human psyche and have influenced how I approach my work with dreams.

Despite important ideological differences between Freudian and Jungian analysis, I have come to believe that these approaches are complementary and require each other in order to achieve a fuller understanding of the psyche. It is primarily for this reason that I have chosen to write this text. Although it is formally an introduction to the initial or *herald* dream in analysis, its broad goal is to illustrate how these different schools of analytical thought can be effectively combined to yield a more effective therapeutic approach.

But before one can integrate these approaches, it is important to understand how Freudian and Jungian schools of depth psychology conceive of the unconscious and its symbolic representations. The first part of this text is devoted primarily to an exploration of these differences. In addition, it attempts to examine how after nearly a century of analytic practice, they can be reconciled with recent observations yielded by neurological and cognitive psychological research.

The remainder of the text is devoted to examining *herald dreams*. But as the approach to the *herald dream* is identical to that of other dreams, this text is also a practical primer of dream interpretation. It aims at demonstrating how dream interpretation can be synthesized with the other transactions of the treatment. For practitioners who may be skeptics concerning the importance of dreams, it is my expectation that this text will dispel their doubts.

Part 1

Dreams
Theory and Practice

CHAPTER ONE

Introduction

I n an essay entitled the *Practical Use of Dream Analysis* (Jung 1961), Carl Jung suggests that:

> The initial dreams that appear at the very outset of the treatment often bring to light the essential etiological factors (of the neurosis) in the most unmistakable way.

Elsewhere in the same essay, he notes:

> Initial dreams are often amazingly lucid and clear cut. But as the work of analysis progresses, the dreams tend to lose their clarity.

To herald means to announce or to foretell. Although dreams may arguably reflect actual precognition, e.g., by predicting a death or a catastrophic event, interpretations based on precognition are generally best avoided in the practice of analysis.[1] The *herald dream*, i.e., the first dream offered in analysis, does not foretell specific events; but it does invariably identify the issues that will subsequently be important in the treatment. By defining the "initial conditions" of the psyche in treatment via an examination of the *herald dream*, it is

often possible with a high degree of accuracy to predict the subsequent "trajectory of the treatment". Admittedly, psychotherapy
is more complex than the motion of a Newtonian particle. But the
herald dream reveals archetypal elements that are subject to the *rules*
of the psyche.

As James Hillman, a Jungian analyst points out in *Dream and the
Underworld* (Hillman 1975), *herald dreams* may occur:

> on the eve of the first session, after the first session, be a recent one
> that the patient recalls, or even one from childhood. They have been
> considered to be of diagnostic and prognostic significance, indicating
> where the problem lies and what is likely to be made of them.

Once the core issue, or the *etiological factor*, as Jung termed it,
has been identified, much of what will subsequently appear in
the treatment follows predictably and can be elucidated within
the transference. For this reason, the *herald dream* has a privileged
position with respect to subsequent dreams.

Many patients report dreams that they had the night before their
first appointment. In such cases, the stimulus of entering therapy
has likely evoked the dream. I view *any* dream that occurs between
the time of initial contact with the patient and the first therapy
session as a *herald dream*. In other cases, the *herald dream* may be
reported weeks, months, or even years into the treatment. But whenever it occurs, it is a purposefully evocative subliminal effort to
engage with the analyst.

The *herald dream* can represent the guiding metaphor for the
treatment. By explicating this dream, and, as importantly, by returning to it during the course of the treatment, both patient and
analyst gain a better appreciation of how the patient's core issues are
transforming. Subsequent dreams can be used to compile a dream
series that amplifies prior interpretations of the *herald dream*.

Dreams have been a topic of interest since the dawn of history.
Whereas the ancients viewed dreams as nocturnal messages from
the gods (Von Franz 1991), from a modern secular perspective this
idea is difficult to accept. A substantial portion of human adult life is
spent dreaming, and an even larger part of the newborn's experience is dominated by dream-like states (Jouvet 1999). Yet, no one has
determined why we dream. Opinions vary considerably concerning

the relevance of dreams, with some holding that they are of no importance, while others view them as the portal to the source of the psyche. This controversy is not new. History suggests that there have always been those who placed little stock in dreams, those who have organized their lives around them, and others who might be termed agnostics.[2]

Hillman has suggested that the message of the dream is distorted when it is translated into the language of waking discourse (Hillman 1975). But engaging the dream in its own domain is an *opus contra naturam*[3] for the waking ego. The ego instead insists that the dream come to it; and this can only be achieved by its interpretation. The aim of dream interpretation is not unique. It can be argued that Freud interpreted dreams in the service of increasing ego consciousness, whereas Jung interpreted them in the service of individuation.

As might be expected, the patterns of dreams must be recognized if they are to be interpreted. Jung viewed the patterns of dreams as *archetypal*; i.e., as aspects of transpersonal human experience that are not primarily dependent on personal history. However, dreams are always personal, as they are dreamt by unique individuals. A comparable situation is encountered in evolution, where genetic changes are primarily responsible for evolutionary changes, but their selection occurs at the level of the individual.

I conceive of dreams as the vectorial product of the *archetypal* and personal forces that govern experience. Personality inheres to dreams and transmits idiosyncratic elements to its *archetypal* underpinnings. The enormous potential for gleaning meaning from dreams is such that when a Talmudic sage took a single dream to two-dozen interpreters:

Each interpreted it differently and all of their interpretations were fulfilled. (Taubenhaus, Wise et al. 1918)

Dreams are expressed as symbols. From the perspective of consciousness, symbols, and therefore dreams as well, represent riddles that concomitantly pose questions while making statements. For this reason, efforts at arriving at *the* correct explanation of a dream are as misdirected as Oedipus' response to the Sphinx,[4] precisely because symbols are not definitive. The waking ego is prone to err in imagining that dreams have linear solutions, but symbols are intrinsically non-linear. Instead, like a differential equation, every dream has a set of possible solutions. For this reason, the meaning of a dream can always be re-visited and re-visioned.

At the turn of the 20th century, Sigmund Freud was convinced that he was poised to solve the important problem of why humans behave as they do. He recognized that there were unconscious psychological forces driving the conscious ego "like a rider on a horse", to use his simile. Freud arrived at this awareness via an analysis of his own dreams. In his landmark work, *The Interpretation of Dreams*[5] (Freud 1900), Freud suggested that dreams were the direct or "royal" path to the unconscious. In a letter to his longtime confidante, Wilhelm Fliess, Freud mused that he would best be remembered by future generations for having unraveled the mystery of dreams.

As a physician,[6] Freud applied his new insights primarily to the treatment of the neuroses. He attributed a key role in the theory and practice of psychoanalysis to dreams and he never deviated from this position.[7] But at the turn of the 21st century, dreams no longer carry the privileged status that Freud attributed to them (Khan 1976). Currently, many practicing psychotherapists have little interest in dreams and limited expertise in their interpretation. Multiple factors account for this change. In most academic medical centers in the United States, psychopharmacological interventions have become the mainstay of psychiatric treatment. When psychotherapies are pursued at all, they are most often short-term cognitive-behavioral treatments. This continues an intellectual tradition that began with the Enlightenment in the 18th century, when religion, superstition, and other imaginal elements were devalued with respect to rational discursive thought.

Cognitive-behavioral approaches place limited value on symbolic thinking. This has led to a general movement away from the examination of the unconscious within psychotherapy, unfortunately at the same time that research has begun to scientifically establish a critical role for subliminal processes. This trend may be ill conceived, as the source of neurotic symptoms, in no small measure, can be attributed to the modern inclination to devalue what cannot be measured or controlled. The cognitive mode of experience has become increasingly important to man. But it remains only one of several modes of human experience. This imbalance between experiential modes contributes to neurotic suffering.

Although dreams exhibit innumerable variations (Van de Castle 1994) certain motifs recur. These include, e.g., dreams of flying, falling, or being chased, to name but a few. A spectrum of feelings has also been reported in dreams, e.g., fear, joy, and sadness. Patients who have suffered trauma frequently report repetitive invariant motifs that tend to recreate the features of the traumatic event.

Other dreams are best considered *iatrogenic*, i.e., they are evoked by psychotherapeutic intervention (Harris 1962). The initial or *herald dream* reported by a patient during a treatment properly belongs in this category. It offers a synopsis of the core psychological conflict that the patient brings to the treatment. When carefully examined, it can yield crucial information with respect to diagnosis, prognosis, and the optimal stance to be adopted by the analyst. For this reason, it is important to recognize the privileged position of the *herald dream* and to make substantial efforts in its interpretation.

Notes

1. Francis Bacon came to the same conclusion in his *Essays* in the early 17th century. On the other hand, Jung in his autobiography *Memories, Dreams, Reflections* interpreted one of his dreams as foretelling the advent of the first World War.
2. Indeed, it might be possible to develop an entire typology based on the perspective towards dreams.
3. *Opus contra naturam* = Work against nature. I have adopted certain Latin terms that recur in Jung's opus in the present text. It is recognized that they are attractive to some but may be off-putting to others.
4. Oedipus is asked by the Sphinx, "what being with one voice has sometimes two feet, sometimes three, sometimes four, and is weakest when it has the most?" Oedipus answers "man" and is spared his life. But the riddle is a symbol that cannot be answered definitively. What Oedipus fails to recognize is that he *is* man and that the answer must include a knowledge of oneself as the Delphian oracle suggested.
5. This work was completed and released in the Fall of 1899 but Freud purposefully had it dated 1900 by the editor in order to herald its importance to the new century.

6. Freud was by training a neurologist and neuropathologist. His primary exposure to psychological problems was via hysteria and other "neuroses". He was not a psychiatrist by training and his exposure to patients with severe mental illnesses was limited.

7. It is not by coincidence that both Freud and Jung emphasized the importance of dreams. They recognized the source of the neuroses as a dissociation between the ego and the symbolic and mythical elements of the unconscious. Both men gleaned their understanding of the psyche by their personal work with dreams and the imaginal contents of the psyche. Their descent into the unconscious proved to be the basis for the remainder of their life's work, something that few subsequent analysts can lay claim to.

CHAPTER TWO

Dreams in Theory

In her book *Dreams* (Von Franz 1991), the Jungian analyst Marie-Louise Von Franz describes how Hannibal, driven by ambition to conquer Rome, misinterpreted the meaning of his own dream the night before a fateful battle, leading to an ignominious defeat. Important scientific insights, like Kekule's recognition of the configuration of the benzene ring, have occurred in dreams. Kekule described the image of a snake in uroboric configuration, i.e., swallowing its own tail. Upon waking, the scientist recognized that the carbon structure must be a closed ring.

Extraordinary works of art have also emerged in dreams. Coleridge's epic poem *Kubla Khan* appeared in complete form in a dream. Coleridge immediately began to transcribe it faithfully upon awakening but the ending was lost when he was interrupted by a visitor at the door.

The importance of dreams has in general depended on their interpretation. But why dreams should be interpreted at all is a question that is rarely addressed.[1] As the desire to discover meaning and to dispel uncertainty characterizes human behavior, it is possible that the obscure nature of the dream itself evokes efforts at its interpretation. But before embarking on how to approach dream interpretation, it is worthwhile to examine what is currently known about dreams.

Sleep and Dreams

The burgeoning field of sleep biology has yielded substantial information concerning the dreaming brain. It has been established that dreams are a regular and periodic feature of sleep. The majority of dreams are reported during rapid *eye movement* (REM[2]) sleep, although dreams may be reported at virtually any point in the sleep cycle. In REM sleep, the brain shows a pattern of electrical activity that mimics wakefulness. Whereas the ocular muscles exhibit rapid jerky or *saccadic* eye movements, peripheral skeletal muscular activities are inhibited. Jouvet referred to this condition as "paradoxical sleep" and suggested that it includes states of mental activity that are distinct from deep sleep and from wakefulness (Jouvet 1999). Most dreams are reported just prior to waking and the average dream lasts for several minutes. Although the phenomenology of dreams has been exhaustively catalogued, no overarching theory of dreams has been developed.

Some eminent neuroscientists, including Francis Crick, the discoverer of DNA and the genetic code (Crick and Mitchison 1983), have suggested that dreams are the brain's way of ridding itself of surplus information—a sort of nocturnal "spring cleaning". Others including Alan Hobson, a Harvard dream researcher (Hobson and McCarley 1977), view dreams as synthetic creations of the sleeping brain. It is extraordinary that such divergent opinions exist amongst respected researchers. It is likely that their disparate views reflect more the differences in the underlying psychologies of these scientists than the importance of dreams.

What a dream *means* is beyond our capacity to determine because meaning cannot be established objectively. Nevertheless, most would agree that dreams can serve as effective targets for meaning-laden projections. Suffice it to say that at least some psychotherapists, following in the ancient tradition of dream interpreters, are inclined to detect meaning in dreams (Graves 1924) and to conclude, like Freud, that working with dreams is therapeutically beneficial.

Dreams and Neuroscience

Dreams represent a stream of sensory percepts rooted primarily in inner or *interoceptive* experience. Based on research with cats, Jouvet suggested that the ponto-geniculate-occipital pathways—neural circuits critical for visual information processing—play a dominant role in dreams. But the spectrum of sensory experiences reported in human dreams requires contributions from virtually all of the neural areas that register sensation. It has been empirically demonstrated that olfactory and taste sensations are not frequently reported in dreams, whereas visual images, tactile sensations and sounds are commonplace (Van de Castle 1994).

Exteroceptive stimuli, i.e., sensory stimuli from the outer world, can be incorporated in real time into dreams, generally as distorted percepts. Freud cites examples (Freud 1900) in which external stimuli were seamlessly incorporated into the dream narrative. Consider the following observation by Hilderbrand, an early dream researcher, quoted in Freud's *Interpretation of Dreams*:

> In former years I occasionally made use of an alarm clock in order to wake up regularly at a certain hour in the morning. It probably happened hundreds of times that the sound of this instrument fitted into along and connected dream, as if the entire dream had been especially designed for it, as if it found in this sound its appropriate and logically indispensable point, its inevitable issue.

The rapidity with which the dream incorporates stimuli from the outer environment indicates how closely linked are the experience of inner and outer events. Infant observation has demonstrated that input from one of the senses can cross rapidly into other spheres of sensory experience. For example, the sight of the mother's face produces immediate proprioceptive changes in the movement of the infant's facial musculature, a phenomenon referred to as cross-modal competence (Schore 1994). According to Kagan:

> Cross-modal competence matures in a major way after six months because the pre-frontal cortex plays an important role in linking information from different modalities, and anatomical links among sensory association areas, the basolateral nucleus of the amygdala

(which contains sensory information from many modalities) and the prefrontal cortex are immature during the first six months.

According to Gerald Edelman (Edelman 1989), the construction of higher order mental experience is dependent on re-entrant processing of information from different brain regions. Dreams emerge as a product of re-entrant processing of distributed memories and cross-modal sensations synthesized during sleep. What is extraordinary about dreams is that these perceptions are knitted together in a manner that is interpretable.

Jouvet echoes the ancient Upanishad texts (Mèuller 1879) in suggesting that the mental states of dreams are distinct from those of dreamless sleep. When dreaming animals are released from the muscular paralysis of REM sleep, they tend to act out their dreams, without awareness of their surroundings. In dreams, subjective consciousness is embedded within a stream of images but it is, concomitantly, dissociated from external awareness. Whereas dreamers seldom distinguish between themselves and the dream-ego in their reports of dreams, the *dream-ego* is not isomorphic with the waking ego. For one thing, the volitional capacity of the dream-ego is limited with respect the waking ego and the dream-ego often appears to be passively going "along for the ride". In truth, it is questionable whether the waking ego is freer to act in its own right than the dream-ego, but most of us are unable to discern this limitation while awake.[3]

Consciousness in Dreams

Despite the fact that one often refers to "dream consciousness", there is no such monolithic phenomenon. Instead, fluctuating levels of consciousness are observed and these convey important information concerning the dreamer. Critical discernment is a feature of consciousness that requires the activities of the left pre-frontal cortex. Normally, during wakefulness, the right and left-brains cooperate by shuttling information between bundles of connecting axons. A variety of interesting observations have been made in patients who have had these connections surgically ablated, i.e., in so-called "split-brain experiments". Although the brain shows substantial redundancy in its hemispheric activities, the right-brain is primarily responsible for establishing the temporo-spatial features and emotional qualities of experience, whereas the left-brain monitors experience for deviations from what is expected. In reality, sensitivity to novelty is far more complex. As Kagan points out (Kagan 2002) the response to novelty is mediated by:

> neuron ensembles in many parts of the brain including frontal, parietal, and temporal areas, and especially the medial temporal area and entorhinal cortices, hippocampus, and amygdala.

When immersed in dream sleep, the level of discernment by the left-brain and the capacity to detect novelty is diminished. As a consequence, the images of the dream play out automatically, and the dream-ego is embedded in the images. Critical discernment of the unexpected may be altogether absent; or it can fluctuate within the dream.

Dreams exhibit a level of absorption that is comparable to what one experiences while watching a movie. In this state, the dominance of discerning consciousness is suspended with respect to expectations, so that one does not question whether what is appearing on the screen is real. As the writer Susan Sontag notes in her monograph *Regarding the Pain of Others*:

> The attack on the World Trade Center on September 11, 2001, was described as "unreal", "surreal", "like a movie" in many of the first accounts of those who escaped from the towers or watched nearby. After four decades of big-budget Hollywood disaster films, "It felt like a movie" seems to have displaced the way survivors of a catastrophe used to express the short-term unassimilability of what they had gone through: "It felt like a dream".

However, the discernment of novelty can intrude into dreams, especially when the dream narrative introduces material that is far removed from the expectations of waking consciousness. For example, I recently had a dream in which my father appeared several years after his death. After my initial happiness in seeing him again, I experienced the cognitive dissonance of realizing that he was in fact dead. The discrepancy became more lucid with my increasing level of arousal, and I awoke shortly afterwards. This is a common occurrence in dreams but its significance has rarely been considered.

The fact that dreams occur when waking consciousness is diminished is one way of understanding Freud's dictum that dreams are the *via regia* to the unconscious. But this is true, not because consciousness is lost—after all we are aware of our dreams—but because a particularly quality of waking consciousness is no longer dominant. Some "thoughtful" dreamers, who exhibit highly developed levels of critical discernment while awake, tend to report dreams that do not differ considerably from the narratives of their waking lives.[4] For these individuals, their level of vigilance persists even during sleep and access to unconscious material is resisted by left-brain dominance. The same individuals often report difficulties in identifying their affect and exhibit obsessive personality styles.

According to Kagan (Kagan 2002), the right-brain elaborates the lower frequency components of an event, whereas the left-brain elaborates high-frequency information in an array of elements. Low-frequency sounds, such as those that are experienced by the fetus *in utero*, may account for the earlier development of the right brain structures. When the infant later encounters spoken language, the underlying tones and rhythm of the voice, i.e., prosody, continue to be elaborated primarily by the right brain, whereas the rapidly changing complexities of the phonemes of the spoken language are elaborated by the left brain, via semantic networks.

Experience is parsed amongst schemata, sensorimotor structures, and semantic networks. Schemata are the contextualized representations of events and the earliest "structures" to emerge from sensory activation. These schemata are likely shared to some extent with other species. However, the ability to construct language-based semantic networks, including conceptual, metaphoric, and abstract thought, is a distinctly human quality, and it may be the root of the neuroses. But it should not be concluded, as is all too often the case within psychoanalytic circles, that the disposition to experience the world primarily via semantic structuring is a defensive neurotic style to isolate affect, as differences in how experiences are processed is a complex issue that can in part be attributed to genetic predisposition, familial predispositions, and cultural tendencies.

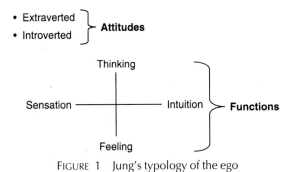

FIGURE 1   Jung's typology of the ego

Carl Jung recognized this when he developed a typology of personality based on the activities of ego-consciousness, in which he categorized thinking as directly opposed to feeling (Figure 1). Jung did not conceive of feeling as an emotion but instead as how the psyche evaluates experience as "good, bad, or neutral".[5] Although criticized for its dichotomous emphasis, at its polar extremes descriptive thinking (semantic representation) does effectively exclude feeling (schematic representation). Excessive thinking can also be associated with an inability to adequately evaluate inner experience, which, in turn, can diminish action, as epitomized by the stasis of Shakespeare's eloquent but ruminating *Hamlet*. In extreme forms, generally associated with organic pathology, the inability to access affect schematas, as Damasio points out (Damasio 2000), can result in a global inability to act.

Dreams and Time

Space and time comprise the dimensionality of our universe. Time can be imagined as linear and directed or as circular. The latter conception is often adopted by myth and ritual, as it emphasizes the repetitive nature of the cycles of the seasons and those of life and death. The circular conception is generally applied to time's passage on a large scale. It achieves hyperbolic proportions in the mythic Hindu concept of the *kalpa*, a mega-cycle of 4,320,000,000 years that culminates, only immediately to begin again. By contrast, the conventional experience of time is linear and sequential.[6] This experience of time leads to the idea of causality, where earlier events lead directly to later ones. Whereas dreams generally represent images in sequence, the idea of "sequential" in dreams does not necessarily mean that causality also applies. Dream actions may or may not follow causally and abrupt shifts in both time and space often occur. This led Freud to conclude that the unconscious has no sense of time.

Modern physics has demonstrated that time and space are relative to objective observers (Einstein 1960). But time is also relative with respect to subjectivity. The philosopher J.T. Fraser (Fraser 1975) categorized time from this perspective.[7] He suggested that time exists as nested interpenetrating *umwelts*. Fraser appears to be positing that changing mental states are associated with shifting perceptions of time. This includes states that are best termed *psychoid*,[8] i.e., beyond psychic registration, as well as those that apply to waking consciousness. Fraser's schema includes four categories of temporality (Table 1). *Atemporality*, in which there is no time or consciousness, may best describe the Buddhist state of *nirodha nirvana*, i.e., temporary mental extinction that has been reported by advanced meditators.[9] This is described as beyond all categories of space-time and is frankly impossible to distinguish from psychological death.

Prototemporality and *eotemporality* represent non-linear modes of temporality that are properly termed psychoid, as they apply to states that are beyond the realm of normal perception. They may correspond to altered states achievable via meditation. Levels of deep absorption or jhanas include experiences in which time dilates and there is "neither perception nor non-perception".

Table 1 The experience of time

• Atemporality	• No time, nirvana
• Prototemporality	• Neither perception nor non-perception
• Biotemporality	• Primary consciousness
• Nootemporality	• Reflective consciousness

Biotemporality applies to what Gerald Edelman has termed primary consciousness (Edelman 1989). *Biotemporality* includes an experience of sequential moments but without the capacity to discern past or future events.[10] It is the consciousness of the present moment, that is commonly achieved in meditation practice. *Biotemporality* is also the dominant temporal experience of dreams, when the dream-ego is immersed in the moment with no awareness of past or future. Freud may have more accurately had *biotemporality* in mind when he concluded that the unconscious had no sense of time.

Nootemporality is as experienced in most moments of waking reflective consciousness. It requires cognitive discernment and the activities of an evolved prefrontal cortex. In *nootemporality*, time is also "tensed" so that past, present, and future are perceived as elements of experience.

Both waking states and dreams exhibit fluctuating mental states that include *biotemporality* and *nootemporality*. For example, in the dream that I described earlier, in which I saw my deceased father, the dream-ego's experience of *biotemporality* was transformed into one of *nootemporality*, as only in *nootemporality* can the distinction between present and past be discerned.

Although we rarely consider it, affects are linked inextricably to how time is experienced. For example, anxiety dreams always indicate fear of what has not yet occurred. As awareness of the future is a feature of *nootemporality*, and anxiety in dreams implies an increased level of discernment by the *dream-ego*, presumably reflecting a relative increase in the activities of the left pre-frontal cortex. The perception of time in dreams also tells us something about its relationship to the "unconscious", for if dreams were an unmodified statement by the unconscious, anxiety dreams could not occur. Instead, dreams must represent a product of altered consciousness, whose accurate relationship to what we imagine to be unconscious is strictly speaking hypothetical.[11] As Freud noted, all mental representations, including dreams are "compromise formations", reflecting a synthesis of the nocturnal activities of the right and left brain, and with varying degrees of primary and secondary consciousness.

References to the *unconscious* will be made throughout this text, in keeping with psychoanalytic tradition. But one must not make the mistake of reifying the unconscious as an actual location in the mind, as opposed to conceiving of it as a set of processes that are subliminal and unavailable to consciousness. In Freud's earlier *topographic* model of the psyche, he emphasized the importance of the preconscious mind that includes contents that can be raised to the level of consciousness. As the psychoanalyst David Shapiro (Shapiro 1981) notes, it is likely that much of what we nominally refer to as unconscious is actually more accurately preconscious.

All models betray the tendency of consciousness to embody abstract processes. Consider, for example, the fictitious model of the atom. No one has ever seen an atom, nor does quantum mechanics suggest that anything like an atom actually exists. Nevertheless, most of us conceive of it with a solid nucleus and orbiting electrons. The psychological inclination to imagine process as things, or as some have put it, verbs as nouns, pervades collective imagination.

This poses its greatest problem in religion. The human psyche is naturally inclined to reify the abstraction of deity. This yields a tendency towards iconography within religious traditions that is perpetually set against opposing iconoclasm. The ancient giant stone Buddhas in Bamiyan, Afghanistan, destroyed by Islamic fundamentalists, have been the most recent well-publicized casualty of this conflict.

The same conflict persists at a psychological level when we refer, e.g., to the "unconscious", as opposed to unconscious process. This tendency has important implications for therapy. By reifying the activities of the psyche, it may be possible to access pre-verbal affect schematas that are linked to images, and that cannot be entered via semantic approaches.

In the ontogeny of the psyche, schematic structures precede semantic networks. We acknowledge the more evolved nature of semantic abstractions in our daily discourse when we refer in somewhat pejorative terms to someone as being "concrete". The fact is that the adult human psyche has difficulty experiencing what cannot be seen or touched, i.e., what cannot be experienced via the senses. Jungian therapy aims at bypassing semantic abstractions by promoting work with dream-images and by encouraging the reification of mental images via painting, sculpture, etc., in order to better access affect directly.

Dreams and the Unconscious

It is impossible to appreciate dreams within the context of depth psychology without exploring the attitudes that Freud and Jung brought to their understandings of unconscious process. The following discussion investigates these differences and how they potentially may be synthesized to yield a fuller appreciation of dreams.

Freud

The ego mediates between the inner world of subjectivity and the outer objective world. But the senses are designed primarily to interface with the outer world. For this reason, interiority is not the primary object of waking consciousness. Psychoanalysis attempts to reverse this process by taking subjectivity as its primary object. Freud aimed at enhancing the ego's awareness of interior experience, as evidenced by the goal of psychoanalysis, i.e., "where *id* (read: unrecognized internal experience) once was, ego shall be".

For classical Freudians, the dream is a manifestation of *id*[12] impulses distorted by a *dream censor* that defends the dreaming ego in the service of preserving sleep. The dream achieves this by *effectively* guising the wishes of the subliminal *id*. As Frank Sulloway emphasizes in his book *Freud: Biologist of the Mind* (Sulloway 1992), Freud was greatly influenced by Darwin and by the idea that the human psyche evolved from a primitive subhuman psychic system the *Id* (It). Freud conceived of *the Id* primarily as the repository of repressed desires that were unacceptable to the acculturated *ego* (I).

For this reason, the Freudian dream conveys its purpose or *telos*,[13] *in potentia*, as the *manifest dream* effectively conceals the *latent dream*. Freud initially conceived of the *latent dream* as a *wish* of a sexual nature. He later included aggression as a feature of the *id*, largely based on his understanding of Darwinian evolution, as dependent on both the reproduction of the species and survival of the fittest.

In order to interpret the Freudian dream, one must identify the *id wishes* by first deconstructing the *dream-work*. The *dream-work* represents a set of mental operations via which a *dream-censor* distorts the *id* impulses. The operations of the *dream-work* include condensation, displacement, regression, reversal, distortion, over-determination, archaization, and symbolization. By recognizing their expression within the *manifest dream*, Freud claimed that the underlying sexual or aggressive wish could be detected.

Freud's concept of the dream effectively turns conventional reality on its head. What is concealed by the dream is the "objective" truth, whereas what is revealed is designed to deceive. This idea is accurately termed paranoid, as one must "know (noia) around (para)" the *manifest dream*, in order to understand its intention. While it is possible that neurotic aspects of Freud's personality predisposed him to be mistrustful, it must be conceded that if the unconscious cannot be known directly, then what is unconscious must by definition be "concealed". However concealment has a variety of implications with respect to consciousness.

The metapsychology of psychoanalysis was derived primarily from clinical observations of hysterical patients. Based on these, Freud concluded that the unconscious was primarily comprised of repressed memories and affects, a sort of underworld dungeon to which unacceptable thoughts and feelings were banished by the acculturated *ego*. This view differs significantly from the modern perspective that conceives of the unconscious as an information processing matrix from which consciousness emerges. In other words, consciousness requires the unconscious for its expression. Whereas Freud alluded to "archaic" aspects within the unconscious that were not primarily attributable to repression, he chose not to explore their contributions to the mind.

The tension between what is revealed and concealed is not original to psychoanalysis. The idea dominates many religious traditions. In the theosophies of the East, including Hinduism, Daoism, and Mahayana Buddhism, what is revealed to man is considered illusory, i.e., *maya*. What can be seen or named is not the deeper reality or "The Way (Dao)", as Lao-Tse states in the Dao Te Ching (Laozi, Ramsay et al. 1993). Western religions also address what is "revealed" and "concealed". In Deuteronomy (29:29), the limits of revelation are expressed as follows.

> The concealed things belong to the Lord, but those things that are revealed belong to us and to our children forever.

If we read this verse as psychology rather than theology, it is consistent with the modern idea that what can ultimately be known by the human mind is limited. We are a product of the functional limits of the psyche. We cannot hear or see outside of a limited spectrum, nor can we directly discern the innumerable physiological activities that are at the core of our experience. In a modern sense, Buddhist psychology recognizes that consciousness is ultimately based in the body. For this reason, many activities that contribute to our experience are beyond discernment. Indeed, psychological analysis may be conceived as a coming to grips with the limits of personal revelation.

Biblical scholars attempted an exegesis of what was concealed by the technique of *hermeneutics*, in which similarities were sought amongst different textual statements. The Talmudists (Taubenhaus, Wise et al. 1918) suggest that several levels of meaning are embedded within biblical text, i.e., they viewed the biblical texts themselves as *symbols*. In fact, Biblical Hebrew, the original language of the Old Testament, is based on a system of three letter consonant roots without vowels. These roots have multiple potential meanings and represent a quasi-symbolic language, so that meaning must be gleaned from the words in context. On the other hand, Greek, the language of the New Testament is based on a primarily descriptive language.

The revealed or *literal* meaning of a verse in scripture corresponds to the *manifest dream* of psychoanalysis. Freud approached the *latent dream* hermeneutically comparable to Aristotle's approach of *similarities*. However, the hermeneutic approach is highly subjective and fraught with difficulties from the perspective of modern science. William James, the father of modern psychology referred to Freud's psychoanalytic approach, as "a dangerous method", because it tends to confuse subjectivity and objectivity (Kerr 1992).

Freud never considered dreams as a creative process, except to the extent that they censored the *id* and he has been criticized soundly for refusing to acknowledge a primary role for creativity in mental life. However, in adopting this stance, Freud remained true to his theory of the neuroses. In this, creativity and play could only represent sublimations of the insistent biological motivations to procreate or to aggress against others. As Sulloway suggests, Freud's sexual theory is best described as psychological Darwinism.

Freud initially dismissed as spiritual occultism the possibility that procreation might itself be the biological aspect of a greater universal law that governs creation and destruction. But as a result of clinical disappointments with patients exhibiting self-destructive and repetitive behaviors, Freud in *Beyond the Pleasure Principle* ((Freud 1920), developed a model of the psyche in which two supraordinate instincts of creation and destruction as *Eros* and *Thanatos* were engaged in perpetual struggle. In so doing, Freud had unwittingly adopted the ancient beliefs of Hinduism, where the universe is the result of endless cycles of creation (Brahma), preservation (Vishnu), and destruction (Siva). However, by this time the majority of Freud's followers were entrenched in the "pleasure principle" and they effectively resisted the Master's "new" heterodox view.

Jung

Carl Jung (Figure 2) was an early protégé of Freud's, who developed a school of depth psychology that continues to adopt dream interpretation as its major therapeutic approach. Jung was a trained psychiatrist, who took exception to Freud's view of the unconscious as both too limited and pessimistic.[14] But despite Jung's desire to be independent of Freud, the school of psychology that he developed

FIGURE 2   Carl Jung

termed *analytic* or *complex* psychology,[15] shares many features with psychoanalysis. Jung, like Freud and other scientists of the day, was greatly influenced by Darwin. Neurotic conflict, according to Jung, was caused by a split between the ego and the unconscious that left the unconscious inadequately represented within the psychic economy. Jung saw this split not only as a consequence of repression but also as the result of societal influences. This can be restated in modern psychological terms to suggest that semantic networks are now the dominant mode of experience, and tend to exclude imaginal-symbolic affect schematas.

Jung posited no *a priori* positive or negative valence to the unconscious. Instead, he conceived of it as an amoral matrix from which consciousness emerges. He further considered the psyche to be a self-regulating system, in which the unconscious compensates or complements the perspectives of the conscious ego, often via references in dreams to what has been excluded from consciousness. In Jung's view, the contributions of the unconscious are potentially therapeutic, as they tend to modify overly rigid and biased perspectives of the ego. The primary goal of Jungian psychotherapy differs from that of psychoanalysis, as the former emphasizes the realization of psychic *wholeness* rather than the overcoming of repression. This is achieved by establishing a new psychic center that is not located entirely within consciousness. Jung identified the *Self* as the actual center of the psyche.

Some of the differences between Jungian and Freudian psychology are more apparent than real. But they do adopt a very different tone in their attitudes towards the unconscious. Freud certainly agreed that the unconscious contributes to our everyday experience. However, the metaphors of psychoanalysis are primarily those of a military encounter,[16] with the unconscious framed as the enemy. One senses in reading Freud that the goal is for the ego to recognize the unconscious, and then to develop mastery over it. Freud's idea of the most advanced psychological achievement is the *sublimation of* the *id*, i.e., the ability to channel *id* impulses towards acceptable societal goals. He concludes that ultimately the reality of the human condition is that we are all destined to suffer but that neurotic misery should be overcome.

Interestingly, Freud's ultimate conclusion is where the Buddha begins with his First Noble Truth, i.e., that all life is suffering (*dukkha*).

But the Buddha sees the possibility of freeing oneself from this suffering by radically deconstructing the self. The Buddhist therapeutic solution, or the Eightfold Path, is designed to profoundly reconfigure the psyche, so that ultimately the psychological illusion of a self no longer exists (anatman), at least as we conventionally recognize it. Buddhism is the ultimate polemic against narcissism.

Neither Freud nor Jung were prepared to go that far, although Jung did incorporate aspects of Buddhist psychology into his theory of the psyche. Jung sought to develop a secular psychology based on the life of the individual, what he termed *individuation*, which was oriented to the underpinnings of the Judaeo-Christian psyche in the West.[17] Rather than mastering the unconscious, Jung fostered an *ego* perspective that demonstrated increased awareness of the unconscious *archetypes*. However, critically and unlike Freud, Jung suggests that the acceptance of a new psychic center, the *Self*, requires faith that the unconscious is nothing other than a part of the *Self*. This acceptance effectively ends the internal struggle that characterizes neurosis. As the *Self* is also equated with the image of God (*imago dei*), it follows that the Jungian system is a religious one in the original sense of the term, i.e., *re ligere*, to re-connect. Like Pauline Christianity, Jung promises salvation via acts (work in analysis) and faith (acceptance of *Self*). Freud rejected this view as illusory.

Structural Models of the Psyche

In the *Ego and the Id* (Freud 1923) Freud (Figure 3) introduced a structural model of the psyche that included the *ego*, the *id*, and the *superego*. This replaced his earlier topographic model of a system conscious, pre-conscious, and unconscious. In the structural model, all of the elements, including the ego are invested with unconscious components. The superego's role is to monitor the ego, and as such it is the source of self-criticism and guilt. Freud postulated that the super-ego was a product of the resolution of the oedipal complex and was yielded by an unconscious identification with parental mores. If harsh or inadequately developed, the superego contributes to the development of psychopathology.

Freud's Structural Model of the Psyche
Superego
Ego
Id

FIGURE 3   Sigmund Freud

The Archetypes

Jung's model of the psyche was also structural, but it was based primarily on symbolic images as they appear in dreams and fantasy experiences. Unlike Freud's model, which is rooted in the potential conflicts between its elements, the Jungian psyche is a "secretory" model, as it posits that contents derived from the deepest levels of the unconscious are progressively modified, prior to emerging into consciousness. Jung postulated that the psyche was primarily organized by a set of unconscious structural motifs that he termed *archetypes* (arche = coming before and typos = form). This idea was borrowed from Plato's idea of the *ideal form* (Cantor, Aristotle et al. 1968) and from Kant's (Kant 1781) concept of the *priori*.[18]

According to Jung, personal experiences are organized by deeper transpersonal motifs. For Jung, the image of one's mother in a dream, or in wakefulness for that matter, was the product of learned associations configured around a deeper mythopoietic image of a

"Great Mother".[19] The idea implies that the mind has evolved expectations of mothering as part of its inheritance and that the *archetypes* reflect this, not necessarily as innate images but as the potential to generate certain images.[20] Jung's concept of the *archetype* as an innate predisposition towards organize experience was considered radical in its time, and even today, psychologists rarely credit Jung with this insight. But few cognitive psychologists would currently argue that the infant's psyche is a "blank slate".[21] As Kagan notes:

> The ability to establish perceptual and visceral schemata, present before birth, permits newborn infants to create schemata for some events in fewer than ten trials. Newborns can discriminate between recordings of their own cry and the cry of another infant . . . Infants are born with biases to attend to particular properties of objects.

Jung recognized that all human experience was necessarily psychological. For that reason, his interests extended beyond psychopathology to include how the human mind viewed the universe and how the psyche and the outer world might be linked. For this reason, his interests in the *archetypes* extended to natural phenomena, some of which cannot be viewed as properly psychological. Jung was attempting to address how the laws that govern the physical world were represented via the activities of the psyche. For example, the fractal rules that describe the fluid dynamics of rivers and the branching of trees also describe the dichotomous branching of neurons, blood vessels, and airways. This could potentially account for the tendency towards dichotomous branching in mental events, what Jung termed the *opposites*.[22]

Jung suggested that the *archetype* functioned along a spectrum that he likened to the electromagnetic spectrum with its poles in both the infrared and ultraviolet. *Archetypes* were expressed both in the outer world and in the human psyche, by virtue of the fact that they represented the natural laws that govern energy and matter. From the perspective of Eastern philosophies, these rules have been referred to as *dharmas*, to be distinguished from the same term that is also used to denote the specific teachings of the Buddha. *Dharmas* are rules for how all energy and matter interact and they extend to the psyche.

Jungian psychology often appeals to religious-minded individuals, scientists, and New Age aficionados,[23] because it attempts
to bridge energy, matter and psyche.[24] However, as Jung pointed
out, as there is no Archimedean point outside of the psyche by
which to make observations, all conclusions about the outside world
are necessarily psychologically-dependent. This does not imply that
there is no world independent of psyche, but it does suggest that
there is no way to appreciate that world beyond the activities of the
psyche. However, the fact that we can, e.g., land a man accurately on
the moon, appears to indicate that our psyche and the outer world
are both governed by the same natural rules.

The Complex

Jung's model of the psyche relies critically on the role of the *complex*.
The presence of complexes was first introduced as a result of Jung's
research with the Word Association Experiment. He noted that
when subjects were given a stimulus word and asked to report a
verbal association to it as rapidly as possible, certain words regularly produced disturbances in the latency of response. These varied
with individuals but they were similar within families. In addition,
these disturbances in latency were associated with changes in heart
rate, respiratory rate, and galvanic skin responses. They affected the
autonomic nervous system, and they are the experimental basis of
what we currently refer to as *affect*.[25] Kagan paraphrases Jung in
modern scientific jargon:

> Because the visceral schemata linked to an emotion are more fully
> represented in the right than in the left hemisphere, it is likely that
> events that engage schemata more often provoke activity in targets of
> the autonomic nervous system

In other words, the *complex*, as defined by the Word Association
Experiment links a semantic network via the stimulus word, to
encoded schemata that are, in turn, linked to autonomic nervous
system activation.

Jung's work stimulated Freud's curiosity, because he saw it as empirical confirmation of his theory of the unconscious and of the neuropathic effects of repression. Jung subsequently developed the theory that mental associations were linked to physical states by complexes and that these were autonomous "splinter personalities". A goal of Jungian analysis was to dissemble the complexes that held sway over the personality. For this reason, Jungian psychology has often been referred to as *complex psychology*. Jung later theorized that the *complexes* were themselves rooted in *archetypes*.

As both personal and impersonal factors contribute to the development of the *complex* and to conscious experience, a crucial aim of Jungian analysis is to become increasingly aware of both. Jung argued that impersonal *archetypal* elements were best revealed by the mythic, imaginal, and artifactual productions of civilization. Awareness of these motifs is as central in a Jungian analysis as is the patient's developmental history. Whereas it is possible to use *archetypal* references to avoid painful personal insights, Jung argued that part of what contributes to personal unhappiness is failing to appreciate that individual psychological life also reflects shared transpersonal experiences, which are the common lot of humanity. The isolation reported by neurotics may at times be greatly alleviated via *archetypal* interpretations.

Jung also viewed his type of analysis as primarily beneficial to patients in the second half of life, a time when questions concerning the meaning of life are often seriously entertained. As in Eastern meditation practices, Jung assumed that a substantial degree of ego stability was present prior to embarking on an *archetypal* analysis.[26] Unfortunately, in modern times, standards of psychological health appear to have changed, so that it is rare to encounter patients who have resolved their "personal" issues at virtually any stage of the life-cycle.

Jung's Model of the Psyche

The elements of Jung's model of the psyche are diagrammed below (Figure 4). They reflect his conception of how the *archetypes* are configured within the psyche based on figures encountered in dreams

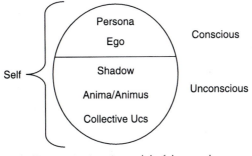

FIGURE 4   Jung's model of the psyche

and in other altered mental states.[27] It is important to note that Jung's model is phenomenological, i.e., it is based on his personal imaginal experiences and on the reported dreams of others. It differs with Freud's model, which is descriptive, conceptual, and abstract.[28]

Persona

As part of consciousness, both *the persona and the ego* mediate with the outer world. *Persona* is the Greek term for the mask worn by players in the theater. Jung recognized that few individuals display the same "face" during all of their interactions.[29] The *persona* is often diagrammatically positioned "above" the ego, because it is constructed, in part, via the influence and expectations of others. For example, were a client to enter a lawyer's office, he or she would most likely be confused and possibly put off if the lawyer were knitting a scarf, because this is not the expected behavior.[30] Individuals who do not effectively assume a specific role in society can be said to have an inadequate *persona*. On the other hand, as Joseph Campbell (Campbell 1988) remarked, if one cannot shed an over-developed *persona*, he or she would be considered a "stuffed shirt". Individuals on both sides of the spectrum of personas abnormality are commonly encountered in psychotherapy.

Winnicott's term "false self" represents the *persona* in defense of the "true self" (Winnicott 1965). Kagan cites the example of two subsets of children who both exhibited a set of distinct objective physiological stress responses that are associated with social-inhibition. One group was behaviorally averse to interaction with laboratory workers, whereas the other was not. It could be said that in the social situation the latter group had adopted a "false-self" affable *persona* in contrast to their anxious "true self". Experiments designed to assess affect based on facial responses have yielded misleading results in persona-conscious Japanese subjects when they are aware that they are being observed. Jung recognized that it is normal to assume different roles at different times, and that it does not necessarily imply an underlying psychological disturbance.

The importance of *persona* is well illustrated in traditional Eastern societies. In the *Bhagavad-Gita*, Krishna emphasizes to Arjuna that it is imperative that he engage in battle against his evil cousins, because, as a member of the warrior class, it is his *dharma*,[31] i.e., his role in society (Mitchell 2000). In structured societies, all members are expected to play at their defined role. But a role can at times conflict with the wishes of the individual. Nevertheless, it is impor-tant to recognize that the importance of the individual is a perspec-tive that developed primarily in the West as part of the legacy of the ancient Greeks (Campbell 1949). After a latent period in the Dark Ages, the importance of the individual again blossomed in the Renaissance and it has persisted in the West, reaching its apogee in the present "Age of Narcissism". The rigid societal norms of the East, where "losing face" continues to be the primary source of shame, can be off-putting to Westerners, who do not value this perspective. Yet, in the traditional East, an individual at odds with society and his or her *persona* is considered to be "nobody".[32]

Ego

The *ego* in Jung's model is a *complex* structured by an *archetype*, as it invariably mediates between the inner and outer experience of the individual. It is the organ of consciousness and includes, according to Jung, the diametrically opposed functions of thinking and feeling, as well as sensation and intuition. The core of ego consciousness contains a lacuna, much like the eye at the center of a hurricane. Like Freudian analysis, Jungian analysis seeks to expand *ego* conscious-ness but as previously noted, its primary goal is the conscious realization of the *archetypes*, not sublimation of the drives.

Shadow

Shadow corresponds roughly to the Freudian—or what Jung termed the *personal*—unconscious. Virtually all of Freudian, and much of Jungian, analysis are based on confronting and re-integrating *shadow*. In its broadest connotation, *shadow* refers to any aspect of psyche outside of consciousness. But as a person is required to cast a shadow, it is generally limited to those aspects of psyche disavowed by *ego* consciousness. The *shadow* has been portrayed many times in literature, e.g., in J.M. Barrie's *Peter Pan* and in Robert Louis Stevenson's *Dr. Jekyll and Mr. Hyde*.

As an unconscious element of the psyche, the *shadow* is susceptible to projection. Most Freudians view projection as a process in which split-off elements of psyche are transferred onto others, as in the transference and in "projective identifications". Excessive projec-tion is observed in patients with rigid *ego* psychopathologies, where there is a harsh super-ego, e.g., in narcissism, paranoia and obsessive-compulsive neurosis. However, Jung recognized that pro-jection is also a normal operation of the psyche, whenever it con-fronts elements in the outer world that are unknown. For example, the Aztecs erroneously "projected" aspects of their mythology onto the Spanish Conquistadors, a mistake that led to the destruction of Aztec civilization. The unconscious itself is the projection of a hypothesis onto activities that we do not comprehend.

Jung chose to illustrate the projective aspects of the psyche via an in-depth examination of its evolution. In his writings, he focused primarily on the role of alchemy to explicate his ideas. Alchemy is widely considered to be the precursor of modern chemistry. At one level this is correct. But Jung recognized that alchemy was also a sophisticated system of thought[33] that served as a philosophical undercurrent within traditional society. The alchemical *opus* was devoted to the parallel transformation of matter and psyche, in an effort to create the "gold" or the *philosopher's stone*. The goal was not merely to produce a precious metal but also to transform the personality into an integrated spiritualized body.

Jung recognized that alchemy was primarily the result of the projection of the psyche onto matter, at a time when virtually nothing was known about the actual structure of matter. Unfortunately, Jung's interest in alchemy has led some to dismiss Jungian psychology as both arcane and superstitious. But it is perhaps more accurate to conclude that Jung's interest in psychology extended into areas of human endeavor that were not primarily medical in nature, including alchemy, parapsychology, physics and religion.

Psychological projections are at the root of conflicts between people, societies, and civilizations. They reach their peak expression during times of conflict, when both sides project their most vile disavowed aspects onto one another. War propaganda is soundly based on exploiting *shadow* projections. These projections are taken to be truths concerning the *other*, which then allows the individual, group, or state, to systematically devalue and kill the enemy without encumbering guilt.[34] To Jung, and to many others, *shadow* is the area where depth psychology and morality rightly intersect. The idea that psychology should be amoral is as impossible as it is unwise.[35]

Anima/Animus

The contrasexual archetypes, i.e., the *anima* and *animus*, have no clear parallel in Freudian psychology. They symbolize a composite symbolic image of the psychological features of the opposite sex. Jung viewed these as "foreign", i.e., as less available to consciousness, and, as such, more deeply unconscious. The role of the contrasexual archetypes has become increasingly controversial in modern times, as differences between the psychologies of the sexes become less defined and perhaps even less politically correct as a topic of speculation. Nevertheless, contrasexual dream figures appear to play an important role in the psyche and in dream interpretation.

Recognizing the *anima/animus* is especially critical for the withdrawal of projections directed at the opposite sex. These projections are the cause of many dysfunctional transactions, including most marital conflicts. They also underlie the tendency to become disenchanted with a partner, when he or she no longer serves effectively as a "hook" for projected fantasies.[36]

Collective Unconscious and the Self

Jung conceived of the *collective unconscious* as the source of the deepest structural motifs of the psyche. It is influenced by innate endowment, as well as societal attitudes and beliefs. One rarely encounters incontrovertible evidence of the innate collective unconscious and independent proof of its existence is controversial.[37] However, there is little doubt that aspects of human unconscious process are shared amongst individuals. Jung cited ethological evidence that newborn chicks respond aversively when confronted with the shape of a chicken hawk's wing. These reflexive instincts are rarely encountered as unsheathed in humans as they are in other animals. Nevertheless, as Pinker points out, the human psyche certainly has certain innate predispositions (Pinker 2002). Kagan captures the unique yet shared qualities of the human psyche as follows:

> Although hominids share many psychological qualities with other primates, evolution awarded our species a number of unique properties. Elaborate semantic networks, a generative syntax, the uncertainty that accompanies detection of inconsistency in those networks, a moral sense, guilt, assignment of self to a web of symbolic categories, and the ability to infer the thoughts and feelings of others are some of the species-specific features that in combination distinguish us from all other animals.

Jouvet gives an interesting example of identical twins separated at birth, who described having identical and recurrent dreams (Jouvet 1999). Melanie Klein (Klein 1984), one of the first psychoanalysts to focus on the psychopathology of children, includes references to innate primitive images within the psyche in her writings. However, whether these images reflect memories of early experience has not been established with certainty.

The supraordinate *archetype* of the collective unconscious, the *Self*, is a unique concept[38] in all of depth psychology.[39] Although Jung in his Collected Works referred to it with a small "s", it has traditionally been capitalized in recent texts, in order to convey its relationship to the God-image. As the dominant *archetype* of the psyche, the *Self* includes both biological and spiritual referents. On one hand, according to Jung, it is the organizing archetype of the individual psyche-soma and I have elsewhere discussed its contributions to psychosomatic organization (Kradin 1997, Kradin 2004). But Jung, influenced by the concept of *Atman* in the Samkhya philosophy of India, also referred to the *Self* as "the center and circumference of a circle", an effort to convey its paradoxical and transcendent features.

The *Self* is the quintessential Jungian symbol. Jung's conception of the symbol includes transcendental implications. In addition to having inexhaustible referents, the symbol, according to Jung, unlike a "sign" points to elements that cannot be defined in conventional terms. This invariably results in a muddled definition that may be off-putting to those who demand precision. This is always a potential problem with the symbolic approach. As the philosopher Michel Foucault notes (Foucault 1994), symbols lead to:

> a self-multiplication of significance, weaving relationships so numerous, so intertwined, so rich, that they can no longer be deciphered except in the esoterism of knowledge. Things themselves become so burdened with attributes, signs, allusions, that they finally lose their form.

But this is precisely the effect that Jung was attempting to convey because for anything to be all at once the center and circumference of a circle, i.e., here, there, and everywhere, demands a willingness to entertain paradox. The same mindset characterizes the Zen *koan*. The *koan* poses an insoluble problem to the Zen adept, until the mind transcends causality and reason, and opens itself to a transcendent experience that cannot be expressed via rational thought. Jung did not view transcendence as beyond the limits of psychology. Instead, he insisted that the mystical experience was a psychological one and differentiated it from theology, which is not a proper topic for psychology.

Jung believed that religious inclinations were an innate feature of the human psyche, as opposed to Freud who dismissed religion as illusion.[40] Jung saw man not only as *homo sapiens* but also as *homo religiosus*. The *Self*, according to Jung, directs the psyche towards the ego towards the recognition of wholeness. For this reason, symbols of the *Self* in dreams and myth connote wholeness, e.g., circles, mandalas, the number "four", precious materials, and specific sectarian referents, e.g., the fish as a symbol in early Christianity.[41]

Jung claimed that the psychological experience of the *Self* is imbued with what Rudolph Otto (Otto 1923) termed *numinosity*, i.e., an affect state associated with mystical or *oceanic* experiences that can be evoked by art, music, nature, ritual, meditation, or via intimate experiences with others. Jung stressed the importance for mental health of a balanced relationship between the *ego* and the *Self*, a concept that Edward Edinger, a Jungian analyst, popularized as the ego-*Self* axis (Edinger 1972).

Jung's theory of psyche was based largely on his study of dreams and on what he termed *active imagination*. The latter represents interactions with imaginal figures while in an altered state of consciousness. In his autobiography *Memories, Dreams, Reflections* (Jung 1961), Jung describes his experiences with an ensemble of imaginal figures that he was able to identify, repeatedly, within dreams and fantasies. He recognized that these figures were symbols that conveyed critical information about his psyche in a predictable manner. His encounters with the unconscious had a powerful and, at times, draining effect on Jung's psyche. Ellenberger (Ellenberger 1970) referred to this period in Jung's life encounters, as a "creative illness", in order to distinguish it from a schizophreniform break. However, it is more likely that this period represented an encapsulated manic-depressive psychosis.[42]

Jung recognized that dreams were an intrasubjective commentary and that certain symbols tended to recur in dreams. These included images of the psychic archetypes, i.e., *ego, persona, shadow, anima/ animus, and Self*. He postulated that by recognizing how these symbols manifest in dreams, it was possible to elucidate the autonomous activities of the psyche. As the activities of the psyche are both *archetypal* and personal, Jung termed their conscious elucidation *individuation* and posited that it was life's primary goal. *Individuation* underscores Jung's belief that neurosis is ultimately an existential issue that cannot be overcome unless the meaning of one's life has been recognized.[43] In a collective sense, Jung believed that man was in a unique position to reflect on his place in the universe because of having evolved the capacity to think and reflect.

Jung believed that it was therapeutically important to transform ideas into images in order to give them form. As previously noted, the tendency to reify concepts is a strong inclination in the psyche. Classical Jungian dream interpretation calls on the dreamer to create pictures and other artefacts that depict dream images, in order to flesh them out into something tangible. Jung recognized through his researches with complexes that affects[44] were associated with images, and that by embodying concepts as images that it was possible to access feelings more effectively. This supports the role of iconography as one gateway to numinous experience.

Jung's approach to dreams is based on his conception of the unconscious. Because the Jungian unconscious is not only a repository of repressed elements, its manifestations, including dreams, don't require disguise. However, the mode of thought that characterizes the unconscious and dreams is symbolic and must be approached differently than discursive thought. Whereas Jung considered dreams to be transparent, their meaning can only be gleaned by those who perceive the implications of symbolic thought. The translation of dream images into the discursive language of the waking ego is best achieved, according to Jung, not by a fixed understanding of dream symbols,[45] or by free-association,[46] but by what he termed *amplification*.

Amplification

Amplification is an exegesis of symbols via their referents. This requires the knowledge of how symbols have historically been adopted in myth, literature, and art (Campbell and Abadie 1974). It also requires the ability to recognize relevant similarities, as Aristotle suggested (Aristotle 1985). As symbols in dreams potentially convey inexhaustible meaning, no single dream interpretation can ever be "correct". Instead, interpretations are selected based on their apparent relevance at the time of interpretation, with the implicit understanding that perspectives on the dream's symbols are likely to change with time. This favors a perspective of *interpretive relativism*, in contrast to Freud's positivistic approach towards dream interpretation.

The technique of amplification "circumambulates" the image,[47] in an effort to expand its potential referents. Unlike free-association, amplification insists on returning to the specific images of the dream. From Jung's perspective, free-association is likely to yield insights that are independent of the dream image. In addition, this approach can theoretically serve to defend against affects that are embedded in the specific dream images. Jung remarked that if a patient dreams of a "deal table", then all efforts must be expended towards understanding why *that* specific table, and not another, was selected by the psyche for its dream narrative.

Notes

1. Rabbi Chrispa in the Talmud expressed his skepticism concerning dream interpretation as follows: "The sadness of a bad dream is sufficient to it, and the joy of the dream is sufficient to it."
2. This is not exactly accurate. Whereas most dreams appear to occur during REM sleep, dreams occur during other stages of sleep as well.
3. Consider the results of the following experiment, in which a subject is told to voluntarily move his arm. Electrodes attached to the musculature of the arm indicate that motor activity begins before the subject is aware of having made the decision to move the arm. It appears that unconscious processing has already prepared the arm for movement before consciousness is aware of its "decision".
4. This is also a relative statement. Dream research demonstrates that the majority of dreams for most people are best described as "mundane".
5. Interestingly, this is how feelings are also defined in Buddhist psychology.
6. I stress the conventional experience as experienced meditators report time and events as moments that come and go without clear continuity, more in line with the idea of time as a cyclic phenomenon.
7. Fraser's text is particularly fascinating. He divides the psychological experience of time into several categories that can be relevant in the practice of psychotherapy.

8. The term "psychoid" was introduced by Eugen Bleuler and appears repeatedly in the works of C.G. Jung. It refers to those aspects of psycho-somatic function that are beyond the range of experience. This would include all that is unconscious as well as the physical underpinnings of the mind. In its broadest sense it also applies to parapsychological phenomena.

9. This begs the obvious question as to whether time exists independent of the psyche. Certainly, there is good *post facto* evidence that there was a time before man arrived on the scene. In physical terms, *atemporality* refers to events prior to the "Big Bang". However, it is meaningless to refer to this as preceding the event as the absence of time means just that.

10. Primary consciousness and *biotemporality* may be seen as the goal of certain types of meditation that promote being in the moment. However, the ability to be in a state of momentary psychology with the capacity for discernment suggests that discernment is a primary quality of primary consciousness. However, the absence of tense implies that this mode of discernment is distinct from what is experienced during secondary con-sciousness. It is apparent that most animals can discern differences with their mode of consciousness, but to what degree they can distinguish past from future is uncertain.

11. Despite the accuracy of this statement, the images of dreams are the product of a mind that does not function by the rules of wakeful-ness. These altered mental states are what analysts refer to as the "unconscious", at least with respect to dreams.

12. The id translates properly to the "it". This level of unconsciousness was impersonal and defied characterization except to say that it is.

13. Jungians are fond of Greek terms. Telos may be loosely translated as "purpose". However, it implies directionality and a goal.

14. Jungians and Freudians habitually dwell on these differences, whereas academic psychiatry has long dismissed much of both Freud's and Jung's ideas as scientifically untenable.

15. I have often wondered why someone with Jung's degree of imagination would merely reverse the term "psychoanalysis" to "analytic psych-ology" in describing his school of depth psychology. One may wonder whether it suggests his continued struggle with Freud for whose vision psycho of analysis was "legitimate".

16. Freud was a devotee of military history.

17. This term is objectionable on theoretical grounds to many. There are fundamental differences as Freud and Jung recognized in the psy-chologies of Judaism and Christianity. However, as Hillman points out, those of us who live in the West are all fundamentally Christian in the

way we are collectively trained to see the world. Many arguments have been made concerning Jung's anti-Semitism and an endnote is certainly not the place to explore them. However, it is fair to say that Jung's approach to the psyche appears to a melding of Christian and Hindu/Buddhist ideas into a secular psychology, oriented primarily towards Christians who have lost interest in organized religion.

18. Prior to the development of psychology, the science of the mind was the proper object of philosophy and religion. Despite Freud's erudite intellect, he was self-admittedly not steeped in the study of philosophy, whereas Jung was. The direct predecessor of psychoanalytic thought was by consensus Frederic Nietzsche. Despite his widespread fame at the turn of the century, Freud insisted that he had never read his works, whereas Jung quoted Nietzsche extensively.

19. A similar idea is encountered in the work of Melanie Klein who posited the presence of archaic imagery in the infantile psyche.

20. One of the greatest areas of controversy in Jung's theory of archetypes is whether there is an innate image of the archetype. Jung refined his concept of the archetype over many years and ultimately suggested that there was no inherent archetypal image but rather that there was the potential within the psyche to create certain images.

21. Pinker has polemically argued against the politically correct stance adopted by many social scientists with respect to the egalitarian nature of the psyche.

22. This hypothesis is the author's, as Jung was not aware of fractals in his time. However, he was able to intuit their presence and believed that the psyche was structured as *opposites*.

23. The archetype is suggested in the beginning of the Gospel of John as how the word (logos) became flesh. This is essentially the equivalent of how the Old Testament God breathed life into Adam or how the Urey experiments showed that proteins could be formed by a mixture of amino acids via the release of electrical energy. Quantum scientists, such as David Peat, are often attracted to Jung, as he qualitatively appears to be speaking to phenomenon that have been described experimentally. However, the terminology and concepts of Jung are constructed too loosely to be translatable into scientific terms directly. New Age aficionados as a group are often drawn to concepts of energy, e.g., auras, in their approach to the psyche. But their beliefs appear to be more determined by their subjective beliefs than by scientific evidence.

24. A standard and often criticized component of Jungian psychology is the concept of *synchronicity*. By it, Jung suggests that physical events are linked to the psyche via meaning. Whereas it is relatively common to experience events in the outer world as related to one's current situation,

scientific efforts to demonstrate an objective basis for synchronicities rarely support their existence. However, from the perspective of subjectivity they are unquestionably valid.

25. These studies were later to become the basis for the lie-detector test. Jung himself was often called upon by the Swiss judicial system to testify concerning the veracity of witnesses.

26. This is an area of controversy for those who practice Jungian therapy. As many of the patients who seek analysis have not attained a sufficient understanding of their personal issues, larger questions about one's position in the universe can appear irrelevant. It is important for the Jungian analyst to make an objective assessment concerning the state of a new patient's psyche and tailor their approach to it. Jung was very clear about this point.

27. The use of the word "fantasy" is not derogatory. Freud's structural theory as well as all other models is based on "fantasies".

28. To my knowledge no one has ever seen their super-ego, although from a Jungian perspective, one might encounter it embodied as a judgmental figure in dreams.

29. Some individuals are remarkably constant, in how they present themselves to the world. This can be a matter of individual taste with some observers favorably impressed by "down-to-earth" honesty, whereas others might view such behavior as a serious breach of etiquette.

30. The issue is sometimes framed as dilettantism, i.e., "Jack of all trades, master of none". Some elements in society frown on the idea of a "Renaissance Man".

31. This is the third meaning of this ubiquitous term, i.e., as one's obligation.

32. The traditional Hindu wife, who refuses to throw herself on her husband's funeral pyre, is termed "nobody".

33. Sir Isaac Newton, perhaps the greatest scientist in history, was an avid alchemist. His writings on alchemy exceeded his scientific opus.

34. Many studies have examined this progression. In the last century, the extermination of most of Europe's Jewry was preceded by a highly sophisticated propaganda campaign that was based on projecting the most vile characteristics onto Jews. Once the non-Jewish populace was able to accept the diminished status of the Jews as "vermin", it became possible for them to kill them en masse without a sense of culpability. This sequence of events has been repeated several times in the last century, e.g., in Bosnia, Rwanda, and Sudan. It is estimated that more than 25 million people fell victim to genocide in the last century, a truly staggering number.

35. The idea that psychoanalysis should be amoral is a natural extension of

its wish to avoid "suggestion". However, there is no such thing as "amorality" in this work. The psychoanalytical literature is replete with moral judgments that its authors do not appear to recognize as such, consider the average analyst's attitudes about rapists, spousal abuse, child abuse, incest, pedophilia, etc. While it may in theory be possible to analyze an individual without judgment, it is impossible to effect a therapeutic result in that milieu. Much of what we term neurosis, is a defect in character from the perspective of moral philosophy and ultimately needs to be addressed as such.

36. Jung and his wife Emma Jung wrote extensively about the psychology of relationships. Jung in particular noted that the problems in most relationships were stereotypic and were caused by projections that made it difficult to see through to the real partners.

37. It appears that Jung claimed the scientific basis of the collective unconscious on one particular case that he encountered early in his career. He noted that the patient made reference to an image, a solar phallus that appears in Mithraic literature. Convinced that the patient had no access to this arcane literature, he assumed that it was a spontaneous element from the transpersonal unconscious. It is currently unclear what this patient actually knew. Nevertheless, there is good evidence to suggest directly from most life experience that humans share common configurations of imaginal contents.

38. This is not entirely accurate. Bion also introduced the concept of "O" which shares features of the ineffable and mysterious unknown.

39. Eugen Bleuler coined the term depth psychology to generically refer to Freud's psychoanalysis and the Swiss school of analytic psychology.

40. It does not seem to me that Freud and Jung had comparable conceptions of God. Freud's image of God is both anthropomorphic and personal. His God is the traditional one of Judaism/Christianity/Islam and is the prime creator that is distinct from man. Although Jung focuses his attention on Christianity, his views are closer to those espoused in Yoga, the Upanishads, and by Gnosticism. For Jung, God, or at least the image of God, is an integral part of the human psyche and is immanent in the Self.

41. Christ was a fisher of men. At a psychological level, fishing also implies pulling something valuable out of the depths of the unconscious.

42. The reasons for this speculation are as follows. First, the energies that Jung exhibited during his life certainly suggest a level of activity that is beyond those expressed by most. His ideas are at times grandiose and there is a persistent aversion to what is personal, as is often seen in bipolar patients. Furthermore, Jung reported that he slept with a gun by the side of his bed and often contemplated suicide during this period, likely a reflection of severe depression. The loss of his relationship

with Freud and his being shunned subsequently by the psychoanalytic community could certainly represent the precipitating event for a manic episode. However, to simply ascribe these events to Jung's psychopathology misses the fact that he was able to incorporate this episode into the subsequent structure of his life's work. Jung's "creative illness" closely resembles what Eliade describes as the traditional shamanic initiation.

43. Jung stressed the importance of this in his correspondence with the founder of Alcoholics Anonymous. The concept of the "higher power" is conceptually close if not identical to Jung's idea of the *Self*.

44. The term affect is often used in psychology without rigor. It was originally meant to represent those psychophysical responses that "affect" heart rate, respiration, and galvanic skin responses.

45. Jung argued that Freud mistook symbols for signs, i.e., a thing that always stands for another, e.g. cigar = penis, or purse = vagina).

46. Jung took exception to the use of free association in the interpretation of dreams. His position was that free association would invariably lead to one of the sexual complexes that might have no specific relationship to the dream. At an operational level, free-association is by no means easy to do. Despite being instructed not to filter their associations, it may take many years before a patient feels free enough to do so. This makes the value of free-association suspect with respect to dream interpretation.

47. The idea of persistently "circling" the dream image contrasts with the approach of free association which tends to take the dreamer away from the image.

CHAPTER THREE

Dreams in Practice

B y virtue of having trained in both Jungian and Freudian theories and techniques, my approach to dream interpretation represents a melding of both traditions. Whereas I adhere to the Jungian viewpoint that dreams are *transparent*, my application of the insights yielded by dream interpretations tends to focus on personal and developmental issues as well as on their *archetypal* and spiritual implications. I try to orient my interpretations to the sector where personal and *archetypal* experiences intersect, what I term the *zone of individuation* (Figure 5).

Jung justified his emphasis on *archetypal* images by concentrating his practice on patients who had previously been analyzed and who he believed were suffering primarily from existential crises. In my practice, I have encountered few individuals who have adequately resolved their personal conflicts by mid-life, although many patients can work productively in both the personal and *archetypal* areas of experience. In addition, as an analysis progresses, *archetypal* issues seem to arise naturally.

Although Freud's approach to dream interpretation, in theory, appears sound, in practice, it can be unwieldy and arbitrary. In the recent movie "My Big Fat Greek Wedding", the protagonist's father

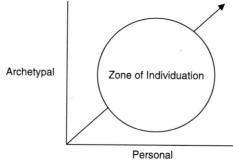

FIGURE 5   The vector of individuation

prides himself on being able to prove that all words are derived from Greek. Using the Japanese word "kimono" as an example, he proves his point via a flawed, yet facile, approach. Freud's ability to demonstrate that dreams are always the result of a disguised sexual wish strikes me as comparable. Wittgenstein expressed his skepticism with respect to Freud's approach as follows:

> He (Freud) wants to say that whatever happens in a dream will be found to be connected with some wish which analysis can bring to light. But this procedure of free-association and so on is queer, because Freud never shows how we know where to stop—what is the right solution. . . . The reason why he calls one sort of analysis the right one doesn't seem to be a matter of evidence. Neither is the proposition that hallucinations, and so dreams, are wish fulfillments . . . This is a speculation.[1]

As will be demonstrated by example, it is possible to arrive at relevant "Freudian" interpretations via an amplification of dream symbols without deconstructing the *manifest dream*. But it would be disingenuous not to admit that there is also subjective choice in Jungian dream interpretation. Currently, the differences between Freudian and Jungian modes of dream interpretation are less than in the past. In recent years, neo-Freudians have focused on the importance of the *manifest dream* (Lewis 1959). Nevertheless, it is generally easy to distinguish Jungians approaches from those of other schools of psychoanalysis, as Jungians are more likely to refer to myths, folk tales, and literature, in their dream interpretations, whereas

Freudians continue to focus primarily on oedipal and transference implications.

The unconscious influence of the analyst on the patient's dreams cannot be underestimated. It is widely reported by clinicians that Jungians tend to receive dreams that exhibit a predominance of *archetypal* imagery from their patients; whereas Freudians receive dreams filled primarily with oedipal referents, guilt, envy, and shame—the staples of the personal unconscious. As most of my patients do not seek me out specifically for my Jungian orientation, the dreams discussed in this text only occasionally exhibited a predominance of *archetypal* images. This makes the challenge of identifying both the personal and *archetypal* elements in dreams challenging and in many respects more satisfying.

Interpretation

One generally considers dream interpretation as the transformation of images into language. In practice, when an analyst listens to the description of a dream, he or she transforms the narrative description into a new set of images based on their own personal imaginings. The evoked images are translated into narrative language, in an effort to confer meaning relevant to the dreamer's current psychological situation.

Whereas the dreamer recollects the images of the dream, the dream interpreter's images represent its re-visioning. This involves a greater degree of freedom than simply recalling the dream and may explain why it is difficult even for experienced interpreters to grasp the meaning of their own dreams. In a recent dream symposium that I gave on this topic, one of the attendees was dismayed to learn that analysts can't interpret their own dreams. As neither Freud nor Jung were formally analyzed except via the interpretation of their own dreams, it is easy to see how this misconception may have arisen. But at the risk of shattering illusions, it is dubious whether anyone can do justice to the interpretation of their own dreams. Having admitted that, it is nevertheless possible to develop a fascination and playful approach to working with one's own dreams, which by itself may be therapeutic. As Foucault (Foucault 1980) points out:

> So many diverse meanings are established beneath the surface of the image that it presents only an enigmatic face. Its power is no longer to teach but to fascinate.

As few are adept at interpreting their own dreams, it stands to reason that dreams may primarily represent a type of intersubjective communication. In traditional societies, individuals with privileged status assumed the role of dream interpreter or alternatively were elevated to positions of importance based on their ability to interpret dreams.

These societies also distinguished those dreams that are personal and of little import for the group at large from those that appeared to shed light on the fate of the community. In *Black Elk Speaks*, a Sioux shaman recounts the dream he had as a young boy that apparently accurately foretold the persecutions of the Ogala Sioux by the U.S. Calvary (Black Elk and Neihardt 1932). As the entire tribe was influenced by the dream, it is an example of what Jung refers to as a "big dream".[2]

As language evolved, the recounting of dreams may have transformed from a direct display of its images, as one perhaps sees in the Paleolithic cave paintings of Europe,[3] to the current description of the dream via discursive language. It is possible that dreams are the remnant of a vestigial proto-language that has been retained during human evolution from a time when the capacity for directed thinking and descriptive language had not yet developed. The development of language was addressed by the literary critic Northrup Frye (Frye 1982), as follows:

> According to Vico, there are three ages in a cycle of history: a mythical age, a heroic age, and an age of the people . . . Each age produces its own kind of language, giving us three types of verbal expression, the poetic, the heroic, and the vulgar that I shall call the hieroglyphic, the hieratic, and the demotic. The hieroglyphic form is "poetic", the hieratic is mainly allegorical, and the demotic is descriptive.

These speculations raise important questions concerning how best to approach dreams in therapy. The usual method is to translate dreams into *demotic* or descriptive language. This is in accord with Freud's idea that "where id (read: poetic/allegorical or symbolic images) once was, ego (read: descriptive language) will be".

However, some dream workers have emphasized the importance of preserving the imagistic quality of the dream without translation. In such an approach, one contemplates the image without describing it. This idea is extolled in Zen Buddhism, where it is encouraged that the organic form of an object be appreciated without critical analysis or a change in its natural context. This idea extols direct schematic experience at the expense of semantic explication.

This alternative approach to dream interpretation adopts an intuitive approach to the images without decoding them. It encourages the dreamer and the analyst to re-experience the dreamscape as a sensation-based schema. My primary exposure to this approach in practice has been through the dreamwork of the Jungian analyst, Robert Bosnak.[4] While I have not routinely adopted it in the analysis of *herald dreams*, primarily because it requires first establishing substantial trust on the part of the analytic couple, it *is* a powerful technique for working with dreams.

A brief summary of this approach is warranted. After an initial telling of the dream, the dreamer is encouraged to re-enter the dreamscape in a hypnogogic state. This is achieved by brief hypnotic suggestion. The goal is to approximate better the mental state within the dream. The dreamer is next encouraged to visualize a specific image from the dream. While in practice any image will do, there is good reason to choose one that appears to convey the maximal affective tension of the dream. Once that image has been conjured, it is reinforced or "embodied", by asking the dreamer to re-experience the sensate qualities of the image, e.g. the temperature, the feeling of the ground underfoot, or some visual aspect of the dreamscape. In so doing, the ethereal image is fleshed out and reinforced as via sensation. The goal is to achieve a schematic appreciation of the image without superimposing a semantic construct. By suppressing semantic networks, it is often possible to engage the affect embedded in the image directly. At times, this can lead to a powerful and transformative catharsis.

It is important for the analyst to appreciate the role of empathy in all modalities of dream interpretation. The psychoanalyst, Heinz Kohut, who developed what is currently termed "Self Psychology", defined empathy as "vicarious introspection". Only by parallel immersion into the dream images can the analyst appreciate the mental states of a patient's dreams. This requires a deep understanding of one's own underlying mental states, as well as openness to the dreamer's experiences. If a picture is worth a thousand words, then it may be said that a dream well-investigated in a therapy hour is worth a thousand hours of conventional verbal discourse.

If interpretation of the dream is the goal, as it primarily is in this text, then the analyst should attempt to adopt a position of "neutrality" when working with dreams. What I mean here is a position "equidistant" between the mental states of the dreaming mind and the waking one. Such a mental state, in Jungian parlance, has been termed *lunar* consciousness, i.e., a reflective state of consciousness that carries less clarity than waking or *solar* consciousness, but that is still capable of engaging in both symbolic and directed thought.[5]

Who is the Interpreter?

Whereas much attention has focused on "who is the dreamer that dreams the dream",[6] less has been written about "who is the person who interprets the dream". For the early psychoanalysts, who focused primarily on a "one-body" psychology, the role of the dream interpreter was primarily to assist the dreamer in recognizing what was being repressed. Although this perspective continues to be a prevalent mode of dream interpretation, intersubjective implications of the dream have increasingly come to the fore.

In practice, dreams may be viewed as having two imaginal axes of reference. The intrasubjective axis links the unconscious with consciousness, whereas the orthogonal axis refers to intersubjective referents. The transference is a special case of the intersubjective axis and one well worth attending to because it is immanent within in the treatment room. For example, a dream that introduces the figure of an angry man may be commenting on an aspect of personal repressed anger, but it may well be directed at the perceived anger of a family member or a transference statement concerning the analyst.

In his *Psychology of the Transference* (Jung 1946), Jung noted that psychological communication occurs concomitantly at a variety of levels (Figure 6). Interpersonal communications can be conscious,

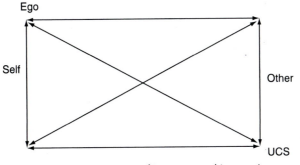

FIGURE 6   Trajectories of interpersonal interaction

directed from one person's unconscious to another's consciousness, or between the unconscious of two people. The latter was Jung's early description of what Klein (Klein 1984) later termed projective identification.[7] It is important to be aware that unconscious communication occurs bi-directionally between the therapist and the patient. This is most likely to manifest via *enactments* that should be monitored by the vigilant therapist.

Resistance to Interpretation

Many patients appear relatively impermeable to information that they perceive as outside of their conscious control, including dreams. They devalue the importance of dreams and postmark them "return to sender". Therapists can also be guilty of returning dreams to their patients "unread". When I have encountered this phenomenon among colleagues and trainees, it generally represents a lacune in their education concerning how to work with dreams. When experience with dream interpretation is limited, dreams can glibly be used to support already recognized elements of oedipal or transference dynamics.

This diminishes the importance of unconscious process and adds little to the treatment. As Jung was wont to suggest, dreams contribute to consciousness by complementing or compensating what is already known. Within the psychic economy, there is little reason to re-state the obvious, unless something has not yet been adequately grasped. When inattention to the dream is limiting awareness, dream motifs will tend to repeat themselves, insistently knocking on the doors of consciousness in order to gain entry.[8] Hillman has suggested that dreams of insects often symbolize efforts by the unconscious to gain access to the dreamer's awareness by "bugging" it (Hillman 1976), thereby exhibiting the instinctual insistence that we associate with insects. When dreams appear to convey the "same old message", it is most likely that the therapist and patient are both missing something important.

The best way to avoid this is for the therapist and the patient to achieve fluency with the symbolic language of dreams. Unfortunately, the symbolic education of psychoanalysts is relatively limited compared to a century ago, when a classical education included an immersion in literature, art, and myth. Trainees often ask me what they can do in order to understand dream symbols better. My response is that symbolic language can best be appreciated by the study of myth, folk tales, poetry, literature, movies, and art. The reader will note that I have not included neuroscience, cognitive psychology, or psychopharmacology, i.e., the current staples of psychiatric education. Although my education as a physician and scientist has been invaluable in my assessments and treatment of patients, it has added little to my ability to interpret dreams or indeed to the recognition of any of the symbolic expressions of the psyche. Perhaps the greatest challenge facing clinical psychiatry and psychology today may be how to preserve an adeptness for working with symbols.

Joseph Campbell remarked that most of what he knew he learned by reading (Campbell 1988). Indeed, working in depth requires an education in depth. A degree in science, medicine, or psychology is a learner's permit and not a license to operate with another's psyche. With respect to dreams, a limited classical education and a training analysis will promote the elementary capacities for working with symbols, but there is simply no substitute for in-depth awareness of how civilizations have adopted symbols over the ages. Consider the potential limitations of discussing oedipal dynamics or narcissism without having ever read the myths of Oedipus or Narcissus. Only an awareness of the complete myth, and often its variations as well, can illuminate the complexities of intrapsychic motifs.[9] It is axiomatic that only a superficial appreciation of the human condition can be gleaned from a limited acquaintance with symbols.

When interpretation is the primary goal of dreamwork, it is necessary to inquire into the dreamer's associations to the dream images. I generally will first ask for the patient's associations to the dream elements, and then prompt him or her to amplify the images. Following Jung, only the specific images of the dream are examined, and any inclinations to develop new images or to pursue associations that are not related directly to the dream images are discouraged. This approach is based on the fact that the dream images have been selected from a large number of intrapsychic possibilities, and therefore they are presumed to be critical for the proper understanding of the dream.

Here, a consideration of the creative arts is relevant. A writer is faced with a potential world of words and ideas but must choose from among them, in order to create a story. The same is true of painters, musicians, and poets. Indeed, all of us are constantly creating specific new ideas, sentences, etc. Alternatively, they may be creating us. It is an indication of the therapist's respect for the dream not to disturb, transform, or re-order its images. The dream interpreter should primarily be an attentive audience. But that includes being comfortable with developing his or her own ideas as to what the dream may mean, without first obtaining the patient's approval. What I am suggesting is comparable to interpreting a work of art without knowing the artist's intentions. Indeed, it can safely be assumed that the artist is never fully aware of its full meaning. The interpretation of dreams should optimally be a dialogue between dreamer and interpreter; one that is potentially enriched by the ideas of both.

I restrict my interpretations to the symbols of the *manifest dream*, as they are of paramount importance in this approach. If a patient dreams of a "dog", then the specific characteristics of the dog should be considered, both in terms of the associations that the patient brings and in the amplification of "dog". For example, is the dream dog a mutt or a purebred? What is its color, its breed?

When it comes to dreams, the devil is in the details. The dreamer may in turn associate to a beloved puppy from childhood or allude to biological, literary, or mythico-religious references to "dogs". All of these are noteworthy and should prompt exploration. But in this approach, the possibility that the image of a "dog" somehow stands for a "cat" or the "analyst" is discouraged, until the reason that the dog image was selected by the psyche has been fully explored.

I find this approach both intellectually satisfying and therapeutic. It serves to counter the unconscious resistances of the patient whose "free" associations can at times lead an inquiry astray rather than be revelatory. Once a dream has been dreamt, it should be viewed as a completed work. Whereas some would object to placing restrictions on the patient's association, it is important to recognize that one important goal of analysis is abstinence. When dreamwork is conducted adeptly, it fosters a middle path between neurotic resistance to creative expression and the naturally unwieldy nature of the neurotic psyche. Like meditation training, one goal of dream interpretation is to yoke the mind in service of expanding its limits.

Introduction to the Dream

Patients may not recognize how working with dreams can beneficially contribute to their treatment. For this reason, the importance of dreams should be explained to a new patient in the early sessions. They should be encouraged to bring dreams to the treatment but should not feel pressured to do so. A therapist who cannot work without a dream is not sufficiently aware that the unconscious is always present in the room. However, the prolonged failure to report dreams in session should prompt an exploration of why this might be the case. Some patients are innately endowed with the capacity for a rich dream life, whereas others are not gifted in this regard. But one rarely encounters a patient who never dreams. As Sir Thomas Browne said:

> That some have never dreamed is as improbable as that some have never laughed.

Patients often ask me how best to remember their dreams. My standard response is that the attitude that they display towards their dreams is most important. If dreams are viewed as inconsequential, they will not be remembered. The ego attends to what it sees as important and most everything else is forgotten. So the most crucial thing is to honor the dream by developing an interest in it. Careful attention to the dream and its details is of paramount importance, for as William James noted (James 1890):

> Millions of items of the outward order are present to my senses that never properly enter into my experience. Why? Because they have no *interest* for me. *My experience is what I agree to attend to.* Only those items that I notice shape my mind . . .

Once that potential obstacle has been overcome, certain techniques can promote the recollection of dreams. Patients should be encouraged to record their dreams in a dream journal, rather than on fragments of paper. This demonstrates a respectful attitude towards the dream that tends to augment recall. It furthermore specifies a dedicated site where a series of dreams can be referred to and compared over time. It is always enlightening to compare old dreams with current ones, in order to see how certain themes may have changed or stayed the same.

Some dreamers prefer to use a tape recorder, in order to capture their dreams. In practice, this is fine, but I generally ask them to make the additional effort of transcribing the dream. The point is that it is more important to exert effort towards the dream's preservation than merely to capture it. Therapy requires work[10] and one way of exhibiting effort is to record one's dreams. In parallel, I document my patient's dreams by writing them in a separate dedicated dream journal at the end of the session.[11] I do not accept copies of written transcripts because I want to convey that I am also prepared to work in the treatment.

Certain patients are prolific dreamers. They regularly bring dreams to treatment, some of them so lengthy and detailed that interpretation is virtually impossible. Whereas this may be a characteristic dream-style for some, it can also represent a resistance to analysis. Patients with passive-aggressive personality styles may bring unwieldy dreams as a negative transference statement unconsciously designed to try the therapist's patience and competence. I gently, but firmly, make it clear early on that only one, or at most two, recent dreams will be considered for analysis in a single hour and that unduly lengthy dreams will not be worked on at all.

Once that message has been received, dreams have a tendency to become shorter and more accessible. Most patients soon recognize how this benefits the treatment.

Having noted that dream styles differ, the implications of this statement should be explored. Dreams are communications that reflect the unique mental processes of the patient. Dream styles are also highly characteristic with respect to their length, subject motifs, and affect. In the same way that a trained philologist can determine whether a play was likely the work of Shakespeare or Marlowe, or that a symphony is the work of Mozart rather than Brahms, dreamers expose their unique psychology via a unique *dream signature*. Changes in this *dream signature* will occur over time in much the same way that one's penned autograph has likely changed since childhood. Changes in the style of a dream are grist for the mill of analysis, as they may communicate change as clearly as the contents of a dream.

The goal of the dream work is to arrive at a balanced perspective that includes both conscious and unconscious positions. Jung conceived of psychological processes as "self-regulating". The psyche from this perspective acts as a gyroscope in an effort to create balance. For example, a patient who is excessively self-deprecating may exhibit overt grandiosity in dreams. The dream often betrays aspects of the psyche that have been excluded from waking consciousness. However, at other times, dreams appear to re-affirm aspects of conscious behavior by complementing them. How to decide which is the case represents the "art" of dream interpretation. The critical point is that dreams can only be optimally interpreted when the conscious position of the dreamer is known.

Notes

1. There is little objective science in dream analysis, and the symbolic approach offered in this text does not claim to arrive at a correct interpretation. Rather, it offers a family of solutions. It is my opinion that the best arbiter of the appropriateness of an interpretation is the analyst's best guess based on his experience with the symbolic approach and his knowledge of the patient's condition. The appropriateness of the

interpretation may be supported by the patient's response that should always include an element of surprise.

2. Black Elk as a young man had what might be termed a schizophreniform experience. In it he dreamt a dream that foretold the destruction of his people by the white man. He participated directly in "Custer's last stand".

3. The cave paintings at Lascaux appear to demonstrate a shamanic character who is the master of the hunt. Shamans have traditionally shared their dreams with tribal societies and it is hypothetically possible that the images exhibited on the cave walls were derived from dream images.

4. Bosnak has written several books about dreams. However, the most detailed description of his approach has recently been published by Janet Sonenberg in her book (Sonenberg, J. (2004). *Dreamwork for Actors*. New York:, Routledge).

5. Both Freud and Jung stressed the importance of two ways of thinking at almost the same times, so it is not possible to determine where the idea actually originated, although Freud did publish his manuscript on the topic prior to Jung. Freud referred to primary and secondary consciousness, whereas Jung termed these symbolic and directed thought.

6. Jung and others have entertained which aspect of the mind is involved in creating the dream. As noted above, I believe that dreams are automatically synthesized by the brain/mind working as an integrated whole as part of its innate propensity to create.

7. It is an unfortunate truth that many of Jung's original descriptions were co-opted by Freudians after Jung's schism with Freud. For the reader who is interested in exploring this area I recommend that they refer to the work of Andrew Samuels (Samuels, A. (1985). *Jung and the Post-Jungians*. London, New York: Tavistock/Routledge).

8. I am not formally considering post-traumatic dreams in this discussion, although what follows probably applies to them as well, as they often indicate a need to process aspects of experience that have been functionally dissociated from consciousness.

9. Graves' opus on the Greek Myths conveys some of the complexity of the situation. Many myths have multiple variants, as do many fairy tales. It is useful to be aware of these as they often shed a unique perspective on a clinical situation.

10. Work = force × resistance.

11. I do this *after* the close of the session and strongly discourage taking notes within the session as it always includes an element of resistance on the part of the analyst.

CHAPTER FOUR

Approaching the Dream

I t is helpful to approach dreams systematically. When patients recognize that the analyst can effectively organize and interpret dreams, they gain increased confidence in the treatment. Dreams generally have a well-defined structure that contributes to their interpretability. Aristotle noted succinctly that dreams have a beginning, middle, and an end (Aristotle 1985). Jung (Jung 1952) suggested that dreams, like a play, can be divided into an *exposition*, (location, time and cast), a *peripetaeia* (plot development), a *crisis* (point of maximal tension), and a *lysis* (resolution).

In practice, patients will often ignore critical details in their reporting of dreams when they first begin working with them. If this continues, it may indicate resistance. After all, when we are truly interested in something, we tend to recall its features in detail. Until that state of mind is achieved with respect to dreams, it is common for the dreamer to report unrelated fragments of narrative that have little coherence. Consider the following dream narrative offered by an intelligent patient who repeatedly expressed doubts concerning the "objectivity" of psychoanalysis.

I was talking on the phone. I had been talking on the phone earlier

Table 2 5 W's of dream narrative interpretation

• Where?	• Dreamscape
• Who?	• Cast of characters
• When?	• Time of dream action
• What?	• Narrative (exposition, crisis, lysis)
• Why?	• Why this dream at this time?

that night. It started to thunder outside. My wife was there. Then I woke up.

I stopped this patient and gently insisted on hearing the details as they developed *in the dream*. As an aid to retrieving and interpreting narrative, I have found it helpful to introduce a modified version of the 5 *W's* of reporting a journalistic narrative (Table 2). A dream has not been fully analyzed until each of the following questions have been asked and answered.

1. *Where* does the action take place?
2. *Who* is in the dream?
3. *When* does it occur?
4. *What* is transpiring?
5. *Why* is this particular dream being dreamt now?

By melding aspects of the journalistic approach with those of dramatic analysis, it is possible to achieve an effective systematization of the dream.

Where

All dreams take place in an imaginal three-dimensional space termed a *dreamscape*. The dreamscape may be the family home, the workplace, or a foreign planet, but there is always a describable space. The dreamscape may persist through the dream or it may change. When it does, it should be noted *how and when* it changes.

The dreamscape is a tangible place. It has physical features and ambiance. All of the experiential sensations that accompany waking reality are potentially available to the dream-ego within the dreamscape. Like a tapestry, it is a *gestalt*—as all of its features are inter-related and contribute to the texture of the dream. At times, recalling even a trivial detail concerning the dreamscape may release the affect embedded within an image. Although most interpreters routinely inquire into how the dreamer "feels" within the dream, this answer may not be as revelatory as the examination of the unconscious affect bound to a specific image.

Who

Like a play, dreams have a cast that is the *who* of the dream. It may include the dream ego, alone, a small number of main characters, or a large supporting chorus. The actual number of characters in the dream, e.g., one, two, three, four, or many, can have important implications for dream interpretation. Patients with introverted personalities frequently report solitary dreams of isolation, whereas extraverts often dream of groups of people. At other times, these situations are diametrically reversed, so that only by knowing the dreamer's waking attitudes can it be determined whether the dream is compensatory or complementary.

The quality of relations in dreams is always informative. For example, two people in the same space who are not speaking with one another indicates something very different than a couple eating dinner together. Dyadic dreams suggest unresolved pre-oedipal issues, whereas threesomes suggest oedipal conflicts. At a deeper level of interpretation, odd numbers of characters may indicate an active dynamic tension in the psyche, whereas even numbers may reflect harmony or stasis.[1]

It is important to determine the gender of dream figures. A colleague once noted that as there are only two sexes, the importance placed on whether figures in dreams are male or female is over-stated. Granted that this is true, an unknown female figure in a man's dream has different implications than an unknown female in a woman's. Heterosexual erotic fantasies, as well as imagined qualities associated with the opposite sex, can be conveyed via a contrasexual dream figure. The dream-ego's relationship to a contrasexual figure may reveal the quality of its relationship not only to members of the opposite sex but also with respect to unconscious affects.

When a dream figure is well known, e.g., a significant other, the projective potential of the figure has already been limited by experience.[2] When a man dreams of his wife, the image will carry specific implications for the dreamer based on his knowledge of her. This is different than encountering a "mysterious woman" in a dream who is unknown to the dreamer. When a well-known figure is encountered, the interpreter is wise not to attribute qualities to the figure that are far removed from the dreamer's awareness.

Isosexual figures in dreams can carry projected contents disavowed by the dreamer. In Jungian parlance, they are *shadow figures*. For example, a quiet frugal man may dream of an acquaintance, who upon inquiry, turns out to be an exhibitionistic spendthrift, qualities that the dreamer consciously repudiates but may unconsciously envy. The *shadow* often takes the form of figures of color in the dreams of Caucasians. The tendency to devalue and stigmatize "the dark side" is a deeply entrenched aspect of the psychology of Western Europeans. Whereas dreamers of color may have white *shadows*, they may also disavow darkness, due to an adoption of white cultural values.

Animals commonly appear in dreams. They may include a family pet or more exotic beasts. Animals often refer to the instinctual life of the dreamer. Certain animals have collectively shared gender connotations. Cats have traditionally been linked to the feminine and dogs to the masculine. Von Franz has suggested that birds frequently imply intuition. Certain animals are linked with the *archetype* of the *Self*, for example the lamb, the fish, and the dove in Christianity. Having noted these possibilities, it cannot be emphasized sufficiently that symbols must be interpreted in the context of the dream and the dreamer, and not isolated from the fabric of the dream. In general, the more distant the animal is from man, phylogenetically, the more deeply unconscious the instinctual qualities that it symbolizes.

When

The *when* of the dream should always be determined. Obviously, it is important whether the dream-ego is represented as a child, as an adolescent, or as an adult. Some dreams take place in the future, although dreams of the past are statistically more common. Some patients dream frequently of childhood or of adolescence. The *when* of the dream can reveal precisely when in development the dreamer's psychic energies were cathected and individuation thwarted. A preoccupation with the past can also be a clue to a depressive propensity on the part of the dreamer, as depressed patients are invariably preoccupied with losses that have previously occurred. Recall that anxious dreams always pertain to events that have not yet taken place, even when they appear to recount past traumas.

What

The *what* of the dream is its story line. In general, dreams display greater levels of activity than are observed during wakefulness. They may include flying, swimming long distances, high-speed chases, and Olympic sexual performances. The dreamscape may shift suddenly, as new characters and challenges confront the dream ego. Other dreams closely resemble the every day activities of the dreamer. Trauma victims characteristically report repetitive dreams, where the scenes, characters, and activities closely resemble actual traumatic events. This theme has been adopted by Hollywood in the production of horror films. However, careful analysis of repetitive dreams rarely confirms invariant details; even small changes may reflect important shifts in the psychological condition of the dreamer and can be an early indicator of therapeutic progress.

If the dream narrative is sufficiently long, the exposition will lead to a *crisis*. The crisis conveys the maximal tension of the dream and also seeks resolution. At times, what should be an obvious point of tension is not reported as such by the dreamer. This may indicate a serious dissociation of affect that is also a core neurotic issue.

Despite the irrational nature of dreams, situations that run totally in the face of common sense can yield clues to the patient's issues. For example, a dream that suggests that the patient has a serious disease that is being treated with a band-aid may imply that the dreamer inappropriately interprets danger or has strong fantasies of an "easy fix" within the treatment. I am reminded of the Monty Python movie, *The Meaning of Life*, in which a 19th century British military officer in Africa has his leg bitten off by a tiger. When asked about what had transpired, he does not know and nonchalantly inquires of the doctor when his leg will grow back, an example of what Charcot described as the "belle indifférence" of the hysterical patient.

Lysis follows crisis, but not always. It is defined as the loosening of a previously bound situation. Although it should be the resolution of the dream, it may at times reflect only a modest decrease in the peak affective tension with no satisfactory denouement. Lysis also occurs via disjunctions in the dream, e.g., "the scene changed; and then I woke up". One is left with the uneasy sense that there is more to come. However, waking may have been the best resolution to the dream at the time. When highly charged moments in the dream are followed by sudden shifts in the dreamscape, it is tempting to suggest that signal anxiety has yielded a reframing of the narrative. But it is impossible to know why these shifts occur and incomplete recall of the dream may account for some of them. As a rule, it is best to. consider them as integral to the dream narrative. However, frequent abrupt changes that yield an unwieldy and confused narrative may reflect resistance to the analysis of the dream.

Why

The *why* of the dream is perhaps the most important question to be addressed, assuming that dreams are relevant to the dreamer's current psychological situation. I raise this question, only after having first worked on the dream, in an effort to stimulate the patient's curiosity, and in hope of potentially developing a novel perspective on the dream. In practice, the response may at times disclose new avenues for analysis, revealed by a casual reference to the day residue or by thoughts and feelings that otherwise might not have been offered.

Notes

1. Whereas statements like the latter may seem odd to those who have not been initiated in the Jungian approach to dreams, clinical experience tends to support such viewpoints. Furthermore, there is increasing experimental evidence that issues of symmetry and harmony have neurophysiological underpinnings.
2. The reader may recall the earlier discussion about projection in the face of what is unknown.

Part 2

Herald Dreams

CHAPTER FIVE

The Centrality of Dreams

T he following *herald dream* of a 17-year-old boy will serve as an initial example. J. was a good-looking, well-dressed, and self-confident young man. He was the son of a powerful local politician and from a large family of brothers and sisters. His mother died when he was a child and his father had subsequently pampered him. His ten older brothers were from previous marriages and his relationship to them was competitive and strained.

He reported the following two dreams that occurred on the same night:

Dream #1: There is a large circle formed by sheaves of wheat. My sheaves are at the center and my brothers' and father's sheaves surround mine and are bowing down to it.

Dream #2: I am at the center of a circle and the sun and the moon and ten stars revolve around me.

When more than one dream is reported from a single night, the dreams are invariably related. They may re-iterate the same theme or, alternatively, they may state a thesis and then counter it with antithesis. It is evident that both dreams have similar motifs. In the first dream, the dream-ego's sheaves of wheat are located at the center of a circle, and his relatives' sheaves surround them and appear to be paying homage. In the second dream, the dream-ego is located at the center of a circle, and the sun, moon, and ten stars surround him. This is an obvious reference to his father, mother, and ten brothers.

The images suggest the *dream-ego's* exhibitionism, grandiosity and entitlement, all characteristics of pathological narcissism. Narcissism is a complex subject that dominates psychoanalytic work. To varying degrees, we all have narcissistic tendencies, as they inhere to the idea of a separate self. Once an "I" is postulated, narcissistic behaviors necessarily follow.[1] Buddhism takes as its final step to Enlightenment the permanent uprooting of greed, hatred and the delusion of being a separate self. This is the ultimate polemic against narcissism and, in truth, perhaps its only cure. For most of us, the distinction between "healthy" narcissism and "pathological" narcissism can be hard to define and largely depends on the level of one's comfort with self and others.

Schwartz-Salant (Schwartz-Salant 1982), a Jungian analyst, addressed this issue in the following argument.

> The narcissistic character structure is found in personalities of widely varying quality. It can be dominant, or an aspect of any psychological pattern. It may be the dominant pattern, in which case we speak of a narcissistic character disorder. It may also be an auxiliary pattern, secondary to another, helpful or destructive to its development.

There is no classical Jungian term for narcissism but many of its features are shared by what Jung termed the *puer aeternus*, i.e., the archetype of the eternal boy. Schwartz-Salant continues:

> It (narcissism) is a strong aspect of the pattern known as the puer aeturnus and its counterpart the senex (old man). It is always a quality in the creative personality, especially evident as that person struggles to bring his or her creativity into the world. It is a dominant quality of the infantile personality with a strong mother complex.

J.'s *dream-ego* is at the center of the world and imagines that this is where others locate him, as well. The persistent need to be the center of attention may indicate a deficit in early mirroring, such as might be expected when a child loses his mother during an early critical period in ego development. This "attention-deficit disorder" manifests as a narcissistically vulnerable personality that defends itself against shame, envy, and fragile self-esteem by projecting these onto others.

However, there is often something genuinely special about the narcissist. As in J.'s case, good looks, intelligence, talent, all seem to accumulate in the successful narcissist. This makes it difficult to sort out what is projected envy from the actual envy of others.

The absence of human characters in both dreams, with the exception of the *dream-ego*'s presence in the second dream, may be interpreted to suggest a defect in the humanizing of internal objects. This can be seen as diminished interest in others, a core feature of pathological narcissism.

Freud judged narcissism (Freud 1914) to be a pathological early libidinal cathexis to the self and argued that narcissists could not be treated by psychoanalysis, as they were unable to develop productive transference responses. Heinz Kohut (Kohut 1984), the psychoanalyst who pioneered the field of Self Psychology, modified Freud's position to suggest that narcissists can generate transference responses, but that these transferences are unconsciously intended to evoke the attention and admiration of the analyst, as compensation for their inadequate presence in development.[2] Kohut termed these *mirroring* and *idealizing* transferences, and argued that the analyst's optimal stance was to serve as a *self-object*, i.e. as a person whose primary role was to attend selflessly to the early psychological requirements of the developing child.

Another cardinal feature of pathological narcissism is excessive self-reference. This may be either outwardly expressed in conversation or behavior or inwardly harbored as compulsive introspection. But both betray a preoccupation with one's self and diminished interest in others. It has been my clinical impression that the extreme tendency towards self-reference observed in the dreams of narcissists often reflects actual early physical and psychological isolation of the child. Narcissistically disturbed patients frequently describe spending large amounts of time by themselves, while their caretakers were, for a variety of reasons, otherwise preoccupied, tending their own narcissistic wounds. As a rule that narcissists breed narcissists, making it almost impossible to account for how much of this psychology is rooted in development versus genetic predisposition. According to Ronald Fairbairn (Fairbairn 1990), a pioneer of object-relations psychology, the ego withdraws from the vacuum created by an emotionally-unavailable mother and turns to an inner object. It then attaches to an inner bad object and simultaneously comforts itself by taking a bodily part as an erotic object. This may be by thumb-sucking or by genital masturbation. These activities represent modes of sensorimotor experience that are associated with the generation of early schemata.

Many narcissists exhibit excessive semantic self-reference, either in conversation or in private thought. As language capacities develop, continued isolation and turning away from the outer world leads to a persistent internal conversation, in which the child serves as both subject and object. Compulsive self-reference also substitutes for the presence of another, and like the previously noted repetitive sensation-based behaviors represents an attempt to self-sooth. Unfortunately, these modes of self-referential experience preclude the possibility of developing genuine mutuality.

Up to this point, the personal and developmental features of the dream have been stressed with little reference to its *archetypal* implications. The first dream adopts sheaves of wheat as its dominant symbol. Wheat is required for the making of bread; it is the traditional staple of man's diet. As a product of the harvest, wheat is a nature symbol, associated with the Great Mother, e.g., the Greek Goddess Demeter. The myth of Demeter and her daughter Persephone (Kore) was the basis of the ancient Eleusian mysteries. The myth alludes to the reappearance of the wheat each year via the metaphor of Persephone's winter sojourn in the land of the Dead after having been abducted by Hades, the Lord of the Underworld. In the myth, Demeter searches everywhere for Persephone, grieving inconsolably for her lost daughter. By reference to this myth, the image of the wheat suggests that loss and mourning may have relevance to the dreamer. As noted, J.'s mother died when he was young. The sun, moon, and stars are dominant images of the second dream. In Greek myth, the sun is Helios, a masculine figure. The moon is associated with Hecate, an avatar of the Great Mother. The stars are lesser luminosities. The family is depicted here in mythic rather than humanized terms, suggesting the importance of *archetypal* imagery in J.'s psychology.

In going from the first to the second dream, the dream symbols transform from monomorphic (wheat) to polymorphic (celestial bodies) images. This transformation from an earth symbol to sky symbols accompanies the appearance of the humanized dream-ego. While all of the elements of the first dream are the same, the dreamer's are more worthy of respect. In the second dream, it is the *dream-ego* that commands the attention (mirroring) and respect (idealization) of the family as celestial bodies.

The circle is a key symbol of both dreams. As previously noted, in Jung's psychology, the circle is the primary symbol of the *archetype* of the *Self*. From this perspective, the dream can be interpreted as the psyche's effort to establish a state of wholeness. It may be posited that narcissism is not merely a characterological disorder but also an effort to integrate a psyche previously thwarted in development. Jung first noted this striving by the psyche towards wholeness in his observations of psychotic patients who spontaneously drew circles prior to exhibiting evidence of psychological recovery. He suggested that this behavior reflected an *archetype* that fostered psychic integration, which he later termed the *Self*.

From an *archetypal* perspective, narcissism may be attributed to a split between *matter*, symbolized by the wheat, and *spirit*, symbolized by the celestial luminosities. This can be reframed as a disjunction in the dreamer's relationship to the Great Mother (read matter) and Great Father (read spirit), substituting for the personal mother and father. When parenting has been seriously deficient due to early loss, depression, disease, or parental self-absorption, the parental *archetypes* tend to appear in dreams in non-human or *theriomorphic* form. Parents who were not "good enough" may be symbolized, e.g. as the ocean or the sky, or as in this case, by sheaves of wheat or the sun and the moon. As the reader can appreciate, the developmental and archetypal interpretations tend to complement each other, yielding similar interpretations but grounded in greater depth.

The positive value of narcissism is rarely emphasized by non-Jungians. Otto Kernberg (Kernberg 1997), a Kleinian-oriented psychoanalyst who has written extensively on narcissism, describes the narcissistic personality in globally-negative terms. He emphasizes the narcissist's unusual degree of self-reference, grandiosity, intense envy, shallow emotions, and lack of concern for others. According to Kernberg, these personalities may have the capacity to work well and to be highly creative, but it is only in the service of fulfilling their ambitions and desire for admiration.

Schwarz-Salant (Schwartz-Salant 1982), adopting a Jungian approach, notes that the narcissistic psyche is positioned between the personal and *archetypal* realms and that the proximity of narcissistic ego to the *Self* may account for the grandiosity of these patients. The narcissist's ego is unduly influenced by the *Self*, leading to what Jungians term an *inflation*. When psychosis erupts, as it can for some severely-disturbed narcissists, the delusional patient most often identifies directly with the God-image, reflecting the identification of the ego with the Self and collapse of the ego-Self axis. The idea of man as God was by no means unusual in ancient times but it was consensually limited to the apotheosis of heads of state, e.g. the Egyptian Pharaohs or the Caesars. However, it later became the dominant myth of Christianity, when Constantine adopted the Near Eastern sect as the state religion of the Roman Empire.

According to Schwartz-Salant, a "great man" may be produced when the ego is pushed beyond its usual limits by the *Self*. Obviously, psychopathology is in the eye of the beholder, as a "great man" in the public eye may be an unbearable narcissist in private. However, it is important to appreciate that narcissism potentially has value. And this was certainly the case for the "patient" in this example.

The reader has probably recognized that we have been examining the dreams of Joseph as recounted in the Book of Genesis (Figure 7). As the Tyndale version of the bible (Tyndale and Rogers 1549) puts it,

Joseph was a lucky fellow, and God was with him

a phrase that well captures the positive features of Janus-faced narcissism. In addition, the Talmudists referred to Joseph specifically as a righteous man with strong ethical sensibilities. This certainly contrasts with Kernberg's conclusion that all narcissists exhibit features of sociopathy.

I chose this example because as the first dream reported in detail in the Bible, it is not only Joseph's *herald dream* but also the *herald*

FIGURE 7   Joseph telling his dream

dream of the entire Old Testament. As the story goes, after recounting these dreams to his family, his angry brothers sold Joseph into slavery. Subsequently, during a famine, Jacob and his sons moved to Egypt, where Joseph, unbeknownst to them, now ruled the kingdom as Pharaoh's chief minister, a role that he had achieved by virtue of his ability to interpret dreams. After Joseph's death, the Israelites were enslaved by a new Pharaoh and required to build the pyramids and store-cities of ancient Egypt.

The remainder of the *Five Books of Moses* recounts the Israelite's Exodus from Egypt, their reception of the Ten Commandments at Mount Sinai, and their persistent struggle at relinquishing their materialism and self-interests, in order to serve their God. All religions call for a diminished investment in self and for faith that this will lead to a transformed self that is free of its previous narcissistic preoccupations. In this manner, Joseph's *herald dreams* reveal the core issue of the ancient Israelites and the Old Testament.

The remainder of the present text is devoted to the examination of the *herald dreams* of real patients in therapy. These dreams were selected from six consecutive patients in my practice, in order to represent an unbiased sample, and from a single case of group supervision. Although the issues raised by these dreams may be small in comparison to Joseph's and the Israelites, their *herald dreams* did play a critical role in how their neurotic conflicts were construed and treated.

Notes

1. Narcissism is rigorously addressed in Buddhist psychology, where it is postulated that no formal self actually exists. The concept of *anatman* (no self) follows from the other tenet of Buddhism that all is impermanent. Accurately speaking, the Buddhists are correct as the self is a series of codependent factors that arise together in each successive moment. It is equivalent to saying that there is no nominative self. We all exist only as verbs. Although Buddhism delves into this issue in detail, virtually all of the major world religions promote diminished emphasis on the self and can be viewed as polemics against narcissism.

2. Many Jungians have been attracted to self-psychology, in part because it also deals with the self. It is tempting to consider the Kohutian self as one pole of the larger archetype of *Self*. However the empathic stance that Kohut insists upon does not adequately consider the role of negative affects, something that Jung would not have looked favorably upon.

CHAPTER SIX

Chains

The following is the *herald dream* of a 46-year-old homosexual man, reported six months into the analysis. Ted was a well-groomed middle-aged man who appeared younger than his age. In the first sessions, he seemed anxious and defensive. He reported being unhappy in his heterosexual marriage and expressed an intense hatred of his employer. Despite his chronic disgruntlement, he quickly offered a series of reasons why he could do nothing to change his situation. His dream was as follows:

> I am at the bottom of the ocean, wrapped in chains. In my right hand I hold a gold key that can open the lock and release the chains. But instead of opening them, I throw the key away.

Associations

"Nothing really comes to mind. I was watching a show about deep-sea diving on television the night before."

Early in the treatment, it is important to explain to patients that dreams represent a language that is different from conventional discourse. The new patient should be helped to recognize that the information revealed by dreams is likely to assist in the treatment, and reassured that dream interpretation is not meant to be a source of shame. It is understandable that a new patient would be reluctant to participate in dream analysis, if it leads to embarrassment. As Jung noted, the ego invariably views its encounters with the unconscious as a defeat, because these detract from its sense of omnipotence. However, recognizing this expected decrease in self-esteem, it can generally be modulated by the analyst.

The Freudian approach to dreams implies that the *manifest dream* guises a repressed *id* impulse. This implies that unconscious contents must necessarily be source of shame. When dreams are feared and devalued, it is generally true that all other aspects of interior experience are as well. Feelings and other forms of spontaneous expression are defended against. In the extreme, a morbid dread of the unconscious can indicate a latent psychosis. In some otherwise high-functioning but obviously rigid patients, it is important to consider the possibility that rigid-ego defenses may be serving effectively to ward off psychosis. As a latent psychosis may take time to manifest, if this is a serious concern, it is wise to approach dreamwork cautiously. Sometimes, it is wise to avoid dreamwork, altogether, until the psychological situation is better assessed and the ego is strengthened. Dreamwork, particularly with borderline[1] patients, can lead to the flooding of consciousness by *archetypal* images that are indistinguishable from psychotic hallucinations.[2]

Competitive patients may avoid reporting dreams because the process gives rise to unbearable feelings of envy of the analyst, who may be seen as better able to "read" the language of dreams. This threatens the self-esteem and omnipotence of some patients. They may defensively refer to dreams as "a waste of time" or immediately offer explanations as to what their dreams mean, often by referring to some aspect of their waking lives, without making the effort to explore symbolic references. Some patients withhold important information and offer few helpful associations.

When this is the case, it is important for the analyst not to appear to be overly facile at constructing dream interpretations. Instead, there should be a genuine effort to enlist the patient's assistance in understanding the dream's potential relevance. The resultant "dream-work alliance" promotes the broader therapeutic alliance that is key to establishing the trust required for the success of the treatment.

After the patients' associations have been examined, they should be questioned carefully concerning the *dream-ego*'s feelings in the dream. In my experience, it is unusual to encounter a large variation in the affects reported in a single dream. However, affect intensity can vary; and it is not uncommon to observe unexpected surges of fear or anger. Whenever possible, efforts should be made to link affects to specific dream images, so that they are not left "free-floating".

Where

This dream takes place at the bottom of the ocean. In reality, one cannot get much deeper and it realistically would be impossible to survive at such depths without specialized diving equipment. The discrepancy of this image with reality is noteworthy, as it may indicate that the patient is unable to sense danger and potentially in serious trouble.

What might the ocean symbolize? One pitfall in dream interpretation is to adopt an overly mundane approach to symbols. Jung criticized Freud's inclination to interpret dream symbols stereotypically as signs of human sexuality (Jung 1961). For example, a long tall object invariably would represent a phallus,[3] whereas objects that are containers, e.g. a purse were consistently identified as symbols of the female genitalia (Freud 1901).

Jung argued that symbols have a richer set of implications and that these are best explored by the process he termed *amplification*. The potential relevance of a symbol can transform with time, so that the meaning of the dream is never fixed but is instead in a continual state of flux. At times, recognizing this truth about the nature of the psyche is in itself an important therapeutic insight. When the patient recognizes that nothing in the psyche is immutably etched in stone, then personal transformation is also possible. In order to demonstrate directly how the meaning of dreams continues to transform, the *herald dream* can be periodically re-examined and its interpretations re-visioned during the course of the treatment. Patients are often surprised to see how the same images take on different meanings with the passage of time.

Having warned against taking a stereotypic approach to dream symbols, it is true that certain symbols have been virtually universally adopted by Jungians in their dream interpretations. For example, the "ocean" may have personal connotations for the dreamer and his or her associations will uncover these. However, the "ocean" also objectively evokes an image of great depth and energy for most of us. As Mircea Eliade, a scholar of comparative religion, points out, the ocean is also widely recognized to be the primordial source of life and therefore a symbol of the Great Mother (Eliade 1963).

When interpreting dreams, it can be helpful to divide space imaginally into vertical and horizontal axes. Virtually all dreams can be analyzed along these orthogonal axes, i.e. with respect to either outer *objective* or inner *subjective* object relations. Within respect to the *subjective* axis, the "ocean" with its great depth is a metaphor for the unconscious. It furthermore suggests the deepest strata of the unconscious, what Jung referred to as the *collective unconscious*. As the Great Mother, it is also the *archetypal* matrix of the dreamer's biological mother. Therefore, on the *objective axis*, and metaphorically speaking, the ocean is the dreamer's mother.

This approach suggests how symbols can be worked, in following Aristotle, via a hermeneutic network of similar meanings to yield information that would not otherwise be apparent. For example, if ocean = unconscious and ocean = Great Mother, than the unconscious = Great Mother as well. As opposed to Lacan's theory that the unconscious is structured like a language (Rabaté 2003), the present symbolic approach suggests that dreamer's unconscious may be structured like his mother's. Indeed, the earliest psychological encoding of implicit procedural memories that constitute much of what we term "the unconscious" results from the early dyadic exchanges between the infant and mother (Schore 1994). This observation implies that we may all, regardless of gender, exhibit an inescapable unconscious identification with our mothers.

If we accept these metaphors of "the ocean", then it may be suggested that the action of this dream is occurring outside of consciousness, and related to a deeply unconscious aspect of his relationship to his mother.

When

The dreamer is an adult and not in some other stage of life. This means that the dream reflects his current situation, although its roots are likely to be located in the dreamer's deep and possibly pre-verbal past.

Who

The dream-ego is the solitary subject of the dream. In some dreams, the *dream-ego* is a passive witness to events, but in this one, it is the active subject. This minor distinction can be informative, as it suggests that the dream-ego plays a willing role in what transpires in the dream.

Isolation in a dream informs us about the patient's relational style. The absence of other dream figures suggests that the dreamer's attitude is likely *introverted*. Freud and Jung differed substantially in their views of introversion. Whereas Jung, influenced by Eastern meditative traditions, regarded introversion as a particular "attitude", Freud viewed introversion as a feature of pathological narcissism.

Freud's essay *On Narcissism* (Freud 1914) was written largely as polemic against Jung's position on introversion.[4] But modern psychometric theories of personality continue to include *introversion* and *extraversion* as generic features of personality rather than as diagnostic elements of narcissism or of its absence, respectively. In most instances it may be fair to conclude that uncompensated introversion is a feature of narcissistic psychopathology, but only as long as it is comparably accepted that uncompensated extraversion is also pathological.

From the dream, we may conclude that the dreamer is either simply introverted or alternatively that he suffers from schizoid structuring of the personality. Schizoid personality is the term adopted by the British object-relations school of psychoanalysts to describe a spectrum of personality types that tend to distance themselves from others, including pathological narcissism. On the other hand, the DSM-IV (American Psychiatric Association 1994) follows the trend of American analysts in distinguishing the narcissistic personality from the so-called schizoid personality. This is based on the former's efforts to seek out mirroring attention by a narcissistic self-object, whereas the deeply schizoidal patient generally shows little interest in affiliating with others. At different times, Ted showed features of narcissistic, schizoid, obsessive, and paranoid personalities. From a psychodynamic perspective, it is more useful to conceive of these as a spectrum of personality types characterized by rigid ego defenses that defend along both intrasubjective and interpersonal axes.

Major discrepancies with reality should be noted in dreams because they may reveal aspects of poor reality testing by the ego. As previously noted, it would be impossible to survive under the pressures that develop at the bottom of the ocean. But Ted was used to functioning under enormous external pressures, although he required elephantine dosages of anxiolytics in order to do so. He never questioned whether his persistently high level of stress might have deleterious effects, despite being otherwise obsessed with his health. The dream suggests that the *dream-ego* is capable of withstanding pressures that no one else can, an indication of Ted's grandiosity, as well as how he tended to ignore situations that were potentially dangerous.

Ted was predisposed towards rational thinking and rarely expressed his feelings. His tendency to "isolate" affect was compatible with his obsessive-compulsive behaviors. Indeed, I often imagined Ted as a steel armored robot, a "Tin Man", who like the character in the *Wizard of Oz* was lacking a "heart".

Ted also exhibited a global inability "to read" his feelings (a-lexi-thymia) which included somatic *interoceptive cues*. He rarely noted normal aches and pains; he had never had a headache; and he had not missed a day of work in twenty-five years. He literally viewed himself as indestructible. In Homer's *Iliad*, the hero Achilles is virtually indestructible, because his mother, the nymph Thetis, had dipped him in the river Styx at birth. His only area of vulnerability was the heel that she had held him by during his "baptism". The mightiest of the Greek warriors, Achilles spends years sulking in his tent, in response to a narcissistic slight perpetrated by Agamemnon, the supreme leader of the Greeks, when he insisted on taking one of Achilles' favored maid-servants as tribute.

Ted had also spent years sulking after his boss reneged on a promise. His hatred seemed to have no bounds. The myth of Achilles captures Ted's ego-based heroic stance in the world, his indestructability, as well as his narcissistic vulnerability.

The only form of human life that can survive under water without assistance is the fetus. In keeping with this fact, an alternative interpretation of the dream image is that it represents an aquatic cocoon, in which the *dream-ego* survives immersed in the amniotic fluid of the mother's womb unimpeded by outer reality. The previous *archetypal* reference to the Great Mother as ocean is reinforced by the consideration of the deeply unconscious fantasy depicted by the dream image.

What

The dream is short but lucid. Furthermore, it proved to be a singular statement by Ted's unconscious. Virtually all of his subsequent dreams appeared to re-iterate features of his daily life. This is a critical observation, as some rigid obsessive personalities experience a paucity of dream images. As previously discussed, it is as though the left-brained activities that monitor experience for differences from expected reality extend into dreams, so that few symbolic fantasies are generated. Ted's psyche was positioned on the borderline between neurosis and psychosis[5] and the excesses of his cognitive style were protecting him from psychosis by structuring the immanence of threatening chaos.

This pauci-imaginal dream style might also indicate that Ted was not attending to his everyday life. In fact, he reported a litany of obsessive-compulsive rituals that permeated his day effectively precluding any spontaneous daily experience with his surroundings. It is possible that the dream was conveying this important unconscious fact by adopting conventional themes.

At the bottom of the ocean, the dream-ego is wrapped in chains. Chains are an impediment to movement and limit one's freedom. The solid metal chains contrast with the fluid ocean water. Jung suggested that the unconscious was structured as sets of *opposites* (Jung 1946). This idea is also found in the great philosophies of the

East. The Sanskrit term *dvanda* is the root of many English words associated with the *opposites* and with psychological conflict. These include *doubt, duality, diabolic, dubious,* to name but a few. It is worthwhile to examine how *opposites* appear in dreams. In this case, the solid chains and ocean water apply pressure in concert on the *dream-ego*. What might be expected to be elements in opposition to each other conflate in this dream-image in their effects. This is a symbolic way of indicating that the psychological pressure and escape from freedom are not in conflict but instead are *ego-syntonic*.

It is worthwhile to consider the counter-transference response to the dream at both psychological and somatic levels. As I listened to Ted's recounting of the dream, I became aware of a vague sense of pressure in my chest. It was as if I were also wrapped in chains. I interpreted my discomfort as a projective identification of the pressure that Ted was not able to bear consciously.

Crisis and Lysis

The apparent lack of conflict for the *dream-ego* made it difficult "to feel" the climax of the dream. I took it to be the image in which the *dream-ego* recognizes that it is in possession of the keys to unlock the chains. This is a standard motif in action movies in which the bound hero manages to free himself in the nick of time. Compare this with Ted's dream, in which there is no frenzied activity on the part of the *dream-ego*. Instead, it nonchalantly, and apparently purposefully, discards the key that could have unlocked the chains. Any anticipation of escape and of the exhilaration that might normally accompany being free was altogether absent. I experienced a deep state of hopelessness when I heard this and interpreted it (to myself) as a reflection of Ted's own projected despair and passive-aggression.

It was evident from the *herald dream* that this would likely be a slow and torturous treatment. It was also clear, despite his outwardly cooperative stance, that Ted would be inclined to let me to do all of the work in treatment. The challenge for me was how to adopt a stance that would provide the support that Ted had not received in growing up, without having to make all of the effort for both of us. This would be the only effective way to address his conflicts concerning dependency and counter-dependency.

In his book, *Escape from Freedom*, the psychoanalyst Erich Fromm (Fromm 1941) considers how authoritarian features in the psyche limit the individual's desire for freedom. This psychological theme is commonly observed in patients with self-defeating and masochistic personalities. Ted's homophobic and physically brutal father was an excellent example of the sadistic authoritarian personality that Fromm described. Ted's adult relationships also tended to be with strong men and women who tried to inflict their will upon him, and limit his freedom. His guilt concerning his closeted homosexuality provided further impetus to remain self-imprisoned as penance for this "sin".

Ted could well be described as a martyr. The metal chains in the dream image were a metaphor for his impersonal brutalizing father, as well as an image of his own harsh super-ego, that kept him imprisoned and wracked with guilt. Ted had been raised as a Roman Catholic, although he consciously rejected his religious upbringing. However, as I considered his suffering, I sensed Ted's unconscious identification with the martyred Christ.

The oedipal triad is represented in the dream by the dreamer, the impersonal chains of the father, and the equally impersonal "oceanic mother". Jung introduced the idea of the parental *imago*, i.e., the parental images within the patient's psyche, to psychoanalysis. In the dream, Ted's parental imagoes have no human qualities, consistent with his reports of profound parental neglect. When the parental imagoes have not been adequately humanized by personal interactions, they tend to appear in dreams as theriomorphic *archetypal* images. Metaphorically speaking, Ted had been raised by the "Great Mother and Father".

In Greek mythology, Zeus, the Great Father and head of the Olympian Gods, has Prometheus, one of the Titans, bound in chains to the side of a mountain as punishment for stealing fire from the Gods and giving it as a gift to man. Prometheus's liver is pecked out each night by a vulture, but regenerates by the next day (Figure 8). What was an unbearable and interminable torture could have ended at any time, if Prometheus had apologized to Zeus. But he refused to capitulate, believing that his punishment was unjust. Instead, he chose to endure his miserable fate. In another myth, Prometheus

FIGURE 8   Prometheus Bound

encloses a litany of human conditions in a jar. When the lid was opened by Pandora, the first woman,[6] all but one escapes. All that remained for man was "delusive hope" (Graves 1988). The myth suggests that there is a link between injustice, suffering, and delusive hope.

Like Prometheus, Ted refused to free himself because he believed that he had been treated unjustly. He chose to renounce his freedom in favor of a "higher cause", becoming a living testimony to the injustices he had endured at the hands of what Winnicott (Winnicott 1965) termed less than "good enough" parents. And like Prometheus, Ted's behavior was motivated by "delusive hope".

Themes of injustice and suffering abound in literature and myth. They reflect the deep *archetypal* outrage that adults retain concerning wrongs meted out by parents and others in childhood. This position is implied by what Freud termed "moral masochism". Moral masochists are redeemed by sacrificing their own life in order to provide salvation for others. Prometheus accepted his fate, so that man could prosper. In Charles Dickens's *A Tale of Two Cities*, the drunken lawyer, Sidney Carton, besotted and enamored with Lucy Manet, goes willingly to the guillotine so that her look-alike husband, the French nobleman Charles Darnay can be saved. His last musing is that:

> It is a far, far, better thing I do than I have ever done before.

However, the masochistic position is not purely motivated by altruistic concerns for others. It is concomitantly driven by deep and often unconscious rage and a strong desire to thwart the will of others. Some of our most revered heroes, Gandhi, Martin Luther King, and Jesus Christ, actively chose to accept their lot in order to express their ethical superiority to their oppressors, and so that others might be saved. But it should not be overlooked that in each of these cases a strong opponent was ultimately defeated. Unfortunately, for most individuals, sacrificing one's life, out of stubbornness and moral superiority proves to be a neurotic solution. Few martyrs are victorious except in their own fantasies.

At the bottom of Ted's masochism was the hope that one day his parents would redress their wrongs towards him, as Prometheus waited for the apology from Zeus that never came. It was evident from the *herald dream*, as well as from the subsequent treatment, that Ted would have to let go of this delusive hope, if he were to move to on with his life.

Jung believed that the solution for a neurotic situation was to be found in the conflict itself. For this reason, it is also important to examine the *herald dream* for clues as to how to proceed therapeutically. In the dream, the *dream-ego* holds a gold key in his right hand that can unlock his chains. The image of the gold key contrasts with the blackness of the ocean's bottom. This evokes the alchemists' challenge. The sought-after gold (*philosopher's gold*) is trapped in the worthless devalued blackness (*nigredo*) of the starting material (*prima materia*). The blackness of the *prima materia* can be likened to the darkness of the soul, i.e., depression that motivates an individual to seek therapy. The analytic work is to identify and enrich the gold that is trapped in that darkness.

Despite the fact that the dream-ego chooses to throw the gold key away, it is not necessarily lost. As the chains symbolize the method of punishment by which the dream-ego, like Prometheus, was imprisoned by the Great Father, then the way out of Ted's psychological prison is to use the golden key, a symbol of the *Self*, to liberate himself first from his negative father complex. At that point, he would also be free to leave the murky depths of the Great Mother and to re-enter the world above.

Why

The dream was reported after several months of twice weekly analysis, and at about the time that he was exhibiting increased comfort about coming to therapy. The *herald dream* lucidly demonstrated Ted's core issues and its images would be re-visited repeatedly in the treatment. With time, Ted was able to withdraw his projections of being victimized and to take increasing responsibility for the profound stasis of his life. This involved re-claiming his disavowed hopelessness and anger and developing a relationship to his own power. Change occurred when Ted was willing to accept that his inner experiences, especially his feelings and his dreams, were valuable. As the dream suggested, the initial work was directed towards deconstructing his father complex and it later moved to the more unwieldy task of addressing his deeply unconscious ties to his mother.

Notes

1. I am using the term "borderline" in its sense which is a condition tenuously located between neurosis and psychosis.
2. There is a famous correspondence that took place between Jung and James Joyce in which Joyce questions Jung about the psychosis of the writer's daughter. Jung answers with a simile of a deep-sea diver noting that the diver can only be safely immersed in the ocean depths if his descent is controlled. In psychosis, Jung replied, the descent is too rapid and the patient is overwhelmed by the contents of the unconscious.

3. Recall Freud's tongue in cheek response that sometimes a "cigar is just a cigar".

4. This essay was written shortly after Jung's break with Freud and it appeared to be Freud's first targeted effort to discredit Jung's ideas.

5. I am using this term in its original sense of designating a psychological position that is on the borderline between neurotic and psychotic function.

6. The Mediterranean view of women seems to focus on their troublesome nature. Both Pandora and Eve generate great difficulties for succeeding generations because they cannot control their natural curiosity.

CHAPTER SEVEN

The Cook

T his is the first dream brought by a 53-year-old woman whose chief complaint was difficulty getting along with her co-workers. Jill was an attractive middle-aged woman who might be described as "animated". She reported this dream in the third session of the treatment.

> I am four years old. I am standing in the kitchen of my parents' house attempting to cook an egg. My parents are in one corner of the room and they are paying no attention to me. I am intent on cooking the egg. My parents disapprove. The egg breaks and flows down the side of the counter.

Associations

"This sounds like something I might have done. I was always trying to do things by myself that I was too young to accomplish."

Although Jill's associations to her dream were limited, I sensed that she was at ease working with imaginal material and that she displayed a degree of ego-objectivity that would help in building the therapeutic alliance.

Jill had previously been in treatment with another therapist for several years. She described her experience as pleasant but not very productive. It is advisable to determine a patient's prior exposure to psychotherapy, and to inquire as to whether it was helpful, as well as to why and how it ended. At times, it may become apparent within the first sessions that the patient has prematurely left a previous treatment, in order to avoid working through unresolved issues, and might benefit by returning to it. However, I do not contact previous therapists unless this issue begs for resolution and then only with the patient's express permission. Inquiries may reveal rigid negative transference responses that predictably will be repeated in the new treatment and that could lead to its premature disruption.

Where

The dream takes place in Jill's parents' house. In her recounting of the dream, she did not describe the house as "the one I grew up in". This suggested to me that she perceived her parents' house as separate from her own. Houses are where the private activities of the family occur. In a similar vein, the psyche houses our most private thoughts and feelings. I wondered whether Jill's psyche was still unduly influenced by her parents and not yet in charge of its own "house". In reality, despite a long career and substantial talent, Jill was still renting a small apartment and had not considered owning her own home.

The dream designates a specific location; it takes place in the kitchen of her family home. As her associations revealed little about the family kitchen, collective meanings were entertained. In earlier times, the kitchen was the site of the family hearth, and traditionally where women exercised their greatest influence. Hestia was the Greek Goddess of the hearth, and the mildest and most charitable of the Olympian Gods. The kitchen is the place where heat is used for cooking. Traditionally, it was Athene, who introduced the art of cooking. Psychologically, affects and emotion are the "heat"

responsible for transforming our behaviors, so that from the subjective perspective, the "kitchen" symbolizes the locus of Jill's affects
and emotions.

When Jill was questioned concerning her feelings in the dream,
she reported being annoyed with her parents for doubting her capacities and for not taking an interest in her. Her anger was long-
standing and it had not been adequately addressed in her previous
therapy. I was recently at a gathering of psychoanalysts where the
topic of anger and forgiveness was raised. One of my colleagues
astutely pointed out that the inability to forgive is "characterological". Patients, who describe life-long bitterness, generally have a
host of other narcissistic issues that impede their happiness and
their ability to relate to others.

When

The dream-ego is four years old in the dream. In addition to being
the oedipal period, it is also the time when children begin to
develop language and reading skills. It is noteworthy that there is no
verbal communication between the dream figures. Instead they are
enveloped by a fog of silence, and they communicate their dis-
pleasure via non-verbal cues. During the treatment, Jill was to report
many dreams set at different times in her life, but this was the only
one that specifically referred to her childhood. Its significance was
demonstrated by the fact that most of the issues that we would work
on were rooted in the childhood dynamic symbolized by the *herald
dream*.

Who

The cast of characters represents the basic triad of the family, i.e.
mother, father, and child. Although one could conclude that this is
an oedipal dream, it does not exhibit the typical alliances of the
oedipal period. Jill had been close to her father as a child and she
reported a life-long struggle with her mother, consistent with the

oedipal dynamic. However, the dream shows the child separated from *both* parents, standing apart from them in a state of defiant independence. As in the previous dream, the dream-ego's isolation suggests the schizoid structuring of Jill's psyche. But unlike the previous case, where the dream was devoid of human contact, this dream includes Jill's parents.

Jill had many friends, although, upon inquiry, it turned out that she was not particularly close to any of them. Jung referred to *Eros*, not as a sexual instinct, as Freud did, but as the tendency within the psyche that seeks relatedness. He believed that women were generally better endowed with this quality than men. Unlike women, according to Jung, many men tend to distance themselves from others, preferring to adopt dispassionate and intellectualized stances via what Jung termed *Logos*. Indeed, recent scientific studies have suggested that women may be genetically predisposed to be more related than men, and that this could be adaptive for the survival of the species. But the superficial ease in relationship that some women display can in some cases guise a deeper schizoid structuring of the psyche. This does not mean that female affability is "false", but it does suggest that female psychology may be complex with respect to intersubjectivity. Ultimately, both men and women with narcissistic issues suffer from diminished *Eros*, which roughly correlates with the diminution in *empathy* that is emphasized in the psychoanalytic literature.

Despite the triad of characters, the dream depicts a functional dyad, with the dream-ego at odds with the parental unit, suggesting that Jill's issues may actually be pre-oedipal in nature. Narcissism is generally considered to reflect a disturbance rooted in pre-oedipal dysfunction. In the dream, Jill's parents fail to exhibit positive attention to the dream ego's activities, consistent with an early failure in mirroring.

Kohut observed that narcissistically disturbed patients reported failures by early caretakers to pay adequate attention to them. This may alternate with attention that is inappropriately intrusive, both modes tending to impinge on the developing psyche. This can yield compulsive efforts on the part of the inadequately mirrored child to elicit the attention of others. Jill was frequently embroiled in conflicts at the workplace that were invariably triggered by efforts to elicit the approval of her employers. Unfortunately, her insistence on attracting attention was disturbing to them, as in her efforts she was often outspoken, contemptuous, grandiose, and entitled.

The *dream-ego* furthermore interprets the parental distance in the dream as disapproval. In truth, Jill had long ago accepted that she was unlovable. Fairbairn (Fairbairn 1990) observed that when the parental object is not available that the infant turns inward to provide its own object. This typifies the schizoid or narcissistic stance. He further noted that children invariably interpret the disapproval of their early caretakers as evidence of their own diminished self-worth. As young children are totally dependent on their caretakers for survival, they fear that by blaming their parents, they will irrevocably lose their attention. The child may wish to spurn her caretakers but for reasons of survival cannot.

Neville Symington, a psychoanalyst, suggests in his book *Narcissism* (Symington 1993) that the developmental attitude adopted by narcissists is the rejection of what he terms the *lifegiver*.

> If one accepts the idea of the lifegiver as the source of emotional life and biological survival—that the two are linked— then the self can never effect a total repudiation, and so a split takes place, with one part of the self turning against the lifegiver.

Kohut's model of the development of the self (Kohut 1971) includes an important role for idealization. When it has not been possible to idealize a parent, the narcissistically disturbed child is likely to become contemptuous of others, to display a diminished capacity for empathy, and to become compulsively self-reliant. This is particularly true when the parent's are excessively critical, as Jill's were. The child's insistence on performing the task in the dream despite their disapproval might be viewed as evidence for her need to exert her autonomy but it also captures the dream-ego's developing lack of respect for her parents' opinions. Her strident independence at a young age revealed that she had already determined that she could not expect support from either of them. In Symington's terms, she had turned against the *lifegiver*.

Jill described feeling profoundly disappointed and embarrassed by both of her parents as a child. Her father was described as distant, self-absorbed, and a poor provider; her mother as anxious, needy, and prone to hysterical outbursts, during which she would physically lash out at her children. At the same time, her mother was unduly critical of any signs of exuberance on their part. Jill constantly felt that she was living in a state of psychological and material deprivation and would refer to herself as psychologically "hungry".

At work, Jill was convinced that she was the only one who could get the job done. Not surprisingly, this angered her co-workers, who would withhold positive feedback for her performance. As a result, her life revolved around a dynamic in which her grandiosity and contempt served only to further reduce the attention that she desired.

What

The active content of the dream is limited to the young girl attempting to cook an egg (Figure 9). In waking life, Jill was an avid chef.

FIGURE 9   Egg

However, she rarely prepared eggs and she offered no associations to them.

Eggs are a critical element in female reproduction. They are a woman's contribution to procreation. Jill was menopausal; and this is a time when the woman's complement of eggs has been exhausted. Despite having been twice married and divorced, she was childless.

The egg is a metaphor of Jill's femininity and creative potential. Birth, menarche, childbirth, menopause, and death represent the nodal points in a woman's life. Menopause is the portal to old age, and the losses of attractiveness and vitality that necessarily accompany it. The stages of life, as Erik Eriksson described them (Erikson 1950), must always be considered in the interpretation of a *herald dream*.

Crisis and Lysis

The crisis of the dream is the tense polarization between the child and her parents. The lysis follows suddenly with the breaking of the egg. The dream-ego's creative efforts appear to have come to naught. This motif of failure applied to many of Jill's efforts. Her marriages, friendships, and career, had all failed to materialize into what she had hoped. Although intermittently successful, she often overreached her capacities, as the child does in the dream. These failures contributed to her disappointment and shame, causing her to dread making new efforts.

The source of her self-defeating behavior is suggested by the dream. From the perspective of oedipal dynamics, success at cooking the egg might have driven the wedge between the young girl and her parents. Even now Jill was fearful of being more successful than her elderly mother. The imagined cost of success was retaliation and abandonment, which was still too great a price for Jill to pay.

All patients have feelings about a new treatment. But few are willing or able to communicate these directly. One reason why *herald dreams* are privileged is that they convey instructions from the patient's unconscious concerning which therapeutic approaches to embrace or avoid.

The dream had definite transference implications. It symbolized Jill's hope and dread about the new treatment. On one hand, she hoped to "cook the egg", i.e., to create something out of therapy that might nourish her. At the same time, she feared encountering the disapproval that would again force her to do all of the work by herself. Most of all, she dreaded failure and abandonment. The "egg" breaks in response to the perceived critical distance expressed by the parents. This suggests that analytical interpretations might well feel critical, distancing, and unwelcome.

My challenge was to find a place in Jill's comfort zone, one that was neither intrusive nor distant. Analytical neutrality is a fluid concept that varies based on the patient's previous experience (Greenberg 1991). The dream suggests that if I were to adopt a distant or critical stance that it would abort the process. For this reason, adopting an empathic stance that mirrors the patient while avoiding interpretations is optimal for narcissistic patients, in the early phases of treatment. The point is that *herald dreams* are not only diagnostic; they are also prescriptive.

Why

After working on this dream, I took the opportunity to share with Jill that I recognized her ambivalence about entering a new treatment. This helped break the ice, not the "egg". The egg is also a symbol of the *Self*. It is a circular structure associated with Pagan fertility and the Christian Easter, a metaphor of renewal. Jill's *individuation* had been thwarted by early developmental failures. Nevertheless, the image of the egg in her dream can be interpreted as an encouraging sign of her psyche's continued efforts at healing. Over the next several years, I witnessed Jill grieve multiple future losses, and we explored the inevitable future losses that she would have to endure as she entered the next stage of life.

CHAPTER EIGHT

Bombs Away

This was the *herald dream* brought by a 34-year-old man in the first month of therapy. James was a rock musician who had achieved modest recognition while playing in local bands. He was a physically imposing man who seemed uncomfortable with his large size.

> I am riding in an open Jeep. It is a beautiful day and I am looking at the flowers along the side of the road. Suddenly I hear a loud blast and see a mushroom cloud rising in the distance. I realize that a nuclear bomb has been dropped and that everyone is going to die.

Associations

"I was watching a program on television the other day about the end of World War II. I like driving in the country. That's all that comes to mind."

Freud noted the role of the "day residue" in dreams (Freud 1901).[1]

I must at once express the opinion that some reference to the experiences of the day which has most recently passed is to be found in every dream.

The day residue represents perceptions registered while awake that appear in the dream of the same night. Recent sleep research has demonstrated that patterns of neuronal firing associated with task-specific learning in rodents are specifically re-activated during sleep (Jouvet 1999). This suggests that memory traces encoded during wakefulness can reappear in dreams. In turn, dreams may be recollected upon waking, so there is evidence for bidirectional communication between waking and dreaming modes of consciousness.

Although it is easy to interpret a dream image as a fragment of recent memory, reducing dream elements in this manner is rarely rewarding. Whereas memories contribute to dreams, there is little reason to conclude that when embroidered into the dream narrative that they refer to actual past events. It is more likely that the dreaming mind incorporates recent memories in the service of producing its own symbolic narrative.

As Jung emphasized, when a dream interpretation adds little to what the dreamer already knows, it has likely missed the mark. However, the converse situation, i.e., the possibility that a symbolic image may represent a previously forgotten or repressed memory, must be considered. For example, in some patients who repeatedly describe dreams in which they are separated from others by a window or some other opaque barrier, it may be possible to elicit a history of prolonged infantile hospitalization in an incubator. The key point is that dreams convey something that has not previously been available to waking consciousness.

The modern human psyche continues to exhibit two modes of communication. Waking consciousness is dominated by discursive thought and descriptive language. Language has been superimposed and integrated with a phylogenetically and ontogenetically older mode of information processing that communicates via images and symbols. These activities roughly correspond to the split-brain activities of the left and right hemispheres, respectively. During sleep, when the higher cortical activities of the left brain are diminished, the older mode of symbolic imaginal expression becomes dominant.

As Jung suggested, one important activity of the dreaming "self" may be to contribute to and critique waking consciousness, via what Edinger referred to as *the ego-Self* axis. There is no intrinsic need to attribute mystical characteristics to dream consciousness, other than those that naturally inhere to symbols. The ineffable and numinous qualities of the *Self,* may reflect this pre-semantic imaginal mode of experience.

The dream communicates a symbolic narrative, but few modern dreamers can fully appreciate its significance without assistance. For this reason, it can be a therapeutic error to follow the patient's lead primarily in the interpretive process. Both Freud and Jung recognized this. The primary function of the analyst is to serve as "a bridge" to the patient's unconscious. Jung termed the linking of unconscious process to consciousness, the *transcendent function*. This term is derived from the mathematical expression of a compound function that includes both real and imaginary numbers. Jung's *transcendent function* links the imaginal unconscious to the semantic consciousness of the ego. The analyst mediates the *transcendent function* by offering well-timed verbal interpretations of the patient's unconscious activities.

Trends towards intersubjectivity in analysis have been increasingly inclined to view dream interpretation as an egalitarian exercise. Many therapists are unduly concerned about influencing patients by offering interpretations of a dream. But it is worthwhile to examine how the pejorative view concerning "suggestion" entered psychoanalysis. Early in his career, Sigmund Freud developed an interest in hysteria. In Freud's time, hysteria was a psychosomatic disorder thought to affect women exclusively (Veith 1965). Patients presented to medical doctors with a broad spectrum of bizarre paralyses and tics that could not be explained on an anatomic basis (Kradin 1997).

Pierre Charcot, the pre-eminent neurologist of his day, noted that he could "cure" many of his patients with hysteria via hypnotic suggestion. His lectures and demonstrations of clinical hypnosis were attended by curious physicians, including Freud. However, it turned out that at least some of these indigent women were responding in ways that they thought Charcot wanted them to, partly out of affection for Charcot, and for the fact that he had placed a much needed roof over their heads.

However, Charcot's success in treating hysteria could not be reproduced by others. His work with hysteria became a source of embarrassment for French neurology, prompting public apologies from Charcot's academic successors. It was largely in response to this scandal that Freud abandoned hypnosis in his treatment of neurotic patients[2] and distanced the new "science" of psycho-analysis from any negative aspersions that might be cast on it by the use of "suggestion". Freud proffered an extreme reaction in suggesting that the analyst should be a *tabula rasa* (blank slate) in the treatment, a disingenuous proposal that he surely must have realized was impossible to achieve in practice.[3]

When trainees ask me whether it is acceptable to offer their own interpretations of their patients' dream, my answer is an emphatic yes! But optimal interpretations require empathy and expertise. Few patients benefit from having dream interpretations force-fed. On the other hand, waiting for the dreamer to recognize the meaning of a dream independently is not often productive. As noted elsewhere, the best approach involves the efforts of both the dreamer and the analyst, but with the latter gently but firmly leading the way.

Where

The dream takes place outdoors, in the countryside on a calm beautiful day. The dream-ego is driving an open Jeep without roof or sides. The image of James driving the car, was consistent with his proclivity to be in control. The *dream-ego's* attention is drawn to flowers at the side of the road. Flowers emerge from the earth, and it may be suggested that the *dream-ego* is oriented towards "Mother Earth", another avatar of the Great Mother *archetype* that is the template for the imago of the personal mother. Flowers appear in the spring, as it is the season of renewal. In the Kore myth, Persephone was picking flowers when Hades abducted her to his Underworld kingdom, a possible reference to death in the dream. Narcissus, enthralled with his own image, was also transformed into a flower after death. These *archetypal* references suggest both a negative mother complex, and a fixation on death.

Who

The absence of other characters, once again, points to the solitude of the dream-ego. James' attitude towards people was generally distrustful. He was narcissistically vulnerable, easily angered when slighted, and displayed a pronounced tendency to isolate affect via intellectualization.

James was wary of men and tended to exploit the women around him. His relationships with women were superficial and he was unable to sustain commitments. For example, he reported a series of extramarital affairs, but justified these in claiming that his marriage was "open". However, on inquiry, it was not clear that his wife had ever agreed to that arrangement.

Guarded and secretive to the point of paranoia, James was uncomfortable presenting his dreams for fear that they might reveal unflattering aspects of his personality. He tended to distance himself from men, preferring the admiration of women whom he took as confidantes, thereby repeatedly enacting his unresolved oedipal complex. His strained relationship with his father, a successful lawyer, raised important transference considerations for his work with me. For example, he would become openly contemptuous when I wore a suit to session, exclaiming that he had never trusted men, like his father, who wore suits.

When

The dream takes place in the present. James came to therapy while in the midst of a hostile divorce. He portrayed himself as cooperative, rather than self-serving, by virtue of agreeing to mediate his differences with his wife without a lawyer. He was surprised when this "conciliatory effort" yielded an angry litigious response by his estranged wife.

What

The dream-ego is preoccupied with its surroundings, when a huge explosion disturbs the peace. This motif characterizes the "apocalyptic dream". Apocalypse (*apo calyptein*) is Greek for revelation or disclosure (Figure 10). In biblical terms, the apocalypse is God's revelation at the End of Days. It is also the Last Judgment of man, and allows no further opportunity for repentance. The journalist Paul Berman describes the guiding myth of apocalypse in his recent book *Terror and Liberalism*:

> The myth is the one that you find in the strangest and most thrilling of writings, the Book of Revelations of St. John the Divine. There are a

FIGURE 10   Apocalypse

people of God, St. John tells us. The people of God are under attack. The attack comes from within. It is a subversive attack mounted by the city dwellers of Babylon, who are wealthy and have access to things from around the world, which they trade. . . . There is also an attack from without—conducted from afar by the forces of Satan, who is worshipped at the synagogue of Satan. But these attacks, from within and without will be resisted. The war of Armageddon will take place. The subversive and polluted city dwellers of Babylon will be exterminated, together with all of their abominations. The Satanic forces from the mystic beyond will be fended off. The destruction will be horrifying.

When apocalyptic images arise in dreams, it is important to identify the terrorist in the dreamer's psyche. This requires probing into religious education and beliefs, attitudes towards injustice, the dreamer's relationship to the father, and to authority. It is also critical, in following the myth, to identify the forces that might be perceived as trying to destroy the dreamer both from within and without.

The energy implied by the nuclear explosion in the dream is enormous, and its effects are imagined by the dream-ego as utterly devastating. At the subjective level, this symbolizes a sudden uncontrolled intrusion of strong destructive affect, generally associated with long-standing but only partially effective repression. The anger in patients like this is like the sputtering of an active volcano. Small eruptions guise a greater destructive capacity that insistently seeks discharge. In the transference, this may be a response to the dream-ego feeling threatened by the analyst. The apocalyptic dream may also symbolize the dreamer's unconscious desire to destroy himself, the analyst, and the treatment, all in one fell swoop.

The current DSM-IV classifications of psychiatric disorders in the U.S.A. separate psychopathology along axes that include affect and mood (Axis I) and personality (Axis II). There is a definite reluctance on the part of therapists to label patients with an "Axis II" diagnosis, due to concerns of appearing to be overly judgmental. In practice, the vast majority of patients in psychotherapy are diagnosed with anxiety or mild chronic depression, i.e. *dysthymia*. At the psychodynamic level, these axes are misleading, as they do not convey the inextricable links between personality structure and affect. Personality develops in large measure as a response to the need to modulate affects and mood. Virtually all patients along the narcissistic spectrum of character, including borderline personalities, exhibit chronic depression or dysthymia and have problems with modulating so-called "negative" affects conveyed via anger, hatred, envy, irritability and destructiveness.

James had a rigid ego structure and was prone to both hypomanic and depressive episodes. At times, he would report working tirelessly and described his accomplishments in expansive terms. But these times would alternate with others, when he was thoroughly discouraged and barely able to get out of bed. He seemed unable to modulate his anger and was either overly passive or explosively aggressive. Fearful of losing control, he refused to consider taking anti-depressant medications. James eventually developed a panoply of disabling psychosomatic symptoms consistent with his inability to channel the anger repressed in his body, effectively. These psychosomatic symptoms increasingly took center stage in the treatment until progress ground to a halt.

Large swings in self-esteem and mood indicate a failure of self-regulation. Another musician, Brian Wilson of the rock group *The Beach Boys*, was widely considered to be one of the great innovative songwriters of pop music in the 1960s. He immersed himself in his composing and successfully executed extremely difficult musical projects. But when the public did not applaud his creativity, he fell into a prolonged period of depression, during which he rarely left his bed.

Manic-depressive behavior, according to the psychiatrist Kay Jamison (Jamison 1993) is positively correlated with increased creative activities, and an inordinate percentage of musicians, poets, and other artists, have exhibited clinical features of bipolar disorder. Bipolar disease appears to have a strong genetic predisposition. But failure to regulate mood may also reflect inadequate early containment and affect regulation by caretakers. In practice, it is rare to encounter a patient with bipolar disorder whose mood swings are not directly triggered by a perceived abandonment.

This dream symbolizes a specific psychodynamic motif that should be explored in depth. The explosion takes the *dream-ego* unawares because it has been lulled into a diminished level of vigilance. Pierre Janet, a French psychiatrist and contemporary of Freud's, referred to these mental states as an "abaissement di niveau mental", i.e., a lowering of the level of consciousness that allows previously unconscious images and affects to emerge.

The apocalyptic dream is generally a feature of post-traumatic psychic organization. James reported a variety of traumas in childhood, including a raging father, fraternal sexual abuse, and the bipolar chaotic behavior of a sister. James defended ineffectively against chaotic intrusions by adopting a Panglossian attitude, in which he saw things as globally positive, symbolized in the dream by the pastoral surroundings. This is reminiscent of the "belle indifférence" described by Charcot in his hysterical subjects and later attributed to sexual trauma by Breuer and Freud.

Crisis and Lysis

The sudden explosion represents the peak affective tension of the dream. As the apocalypse is utterly devastating and leaves no possibility of survival, the dream resolves by hopelessness and despair. This is a metaphor for the resignation and depression that follows traumatic loss. For James, this may have been the premature loss of innocence and the emotional abandonment by parents who refused to acknowledge openly the severe dysfunction of the family. In a repetition of these childhood traumas, James tended to destroy his relationships with the people closest to him, and would then lapse into despair and depression.

Why

The *dream-ego*'s infatuation with nature (matter), followed by the destructive mushroom shaped cloud (spirit), is consistent with an archetypal experience of the "opposites" and of the Great Mother and Father. His unresolved oedipal conflicts had left James uncomfortably close to his mother and defiantly in opposition to his father. The nuclear explosion may be interpreted to depict the paternal rage that traumatically separates the dream-ego from its paradisiacal merger with the mother. From the *herald dream*, it is possible to suggest that

James' core neurotic issue was the premature traumatic resolution of the oedipal phase.

This issue was re-emerging in the treatment as his divorce threatened separation from the maternal imago. James was a *puer aeturnus* with overlapping features of Don Juanism, i.e. the compulsive predilection to seduce and abandon women. According to Jung, these are two of the characterological constructs—the third being homosexuality—that are unconsciously adopted by individuals with a negative mother complex.[4] James was unwilling to assume responsibility for his life and he was wasting his life in a series of rock and roll bands that were not destined to succeed, and in a string of superficial and conflicted relationships that also had no future. As the *herald dream* indicated, James' future was bleak.

In his book *Denial of Death*, Ernst Becker points out how much of the neurotic's inability to productively live their life results from their fear of death. Although, James did not discuss this issue frequently, the *herald dream* emphasizes how destructiveness and death loomed in his psyche. As his psychosomatic symptoms increased, James withdrew increasingly from the outer world.

Nevertheless, with therapy, he began to recognize the importance of commitment and how to relate maturely to women. His fear and anger towards his father were tempered. The *herald dream* alerted me to the depth of James' destructiveness and how he would experience me in the transference as a powerful and threatening figure like his father. The dream conveyed how James needed to be more open to his surroundings and to nature, but that he also had to acknowledge that disavowed affects were intrusively destroying his life.

Notes

1. It is only proper to acknowledge that Freud did not invent dream interpretation. There were many scientifically-minded investigators who offered a variety of theories concerning dreams before Freud, some of which are worthy of continued examination.

2. The analytic couch is a remnant of this time. Freud would sit beside the patient, touch their heads, and make hypnotic suggestions in order to

treat them. As a poor young physician, he may not have been able to buy a new couch, so he continued to use it for his analytical work, transforming its function into a place where the patient could now free-associate without disturbance, a sort of therapeutic reaction-formation.

3. There is no question about this, based on the anecdotes told by some of Freud's patients. He was at times far from being a blank slate and actually engaged in social discourse and business dealings with some of his patients.

4. Jung suggested that men with a strong unresolved mother complex would either develop along archetypal lines as a *puer aeturnus*, a Don Juan, or a homosexual.

CHAPTER NINE

Shadowlands

This was the first dream of a 38-year-old man who presented with panic attacks and depression. Bob appeared modestly disheveled, and was nursing a beerbelly. He oscillated in his demeanor from shy and retiring to overconfident and overbearing. He had been referred to therapy because of difficulties with unexpressed anger. He reported his initial dream approximately one year into the treatment.

> I am at college but I am trying to go home. I get on the wrong train and wind up in a black neighborhood. A black man approaches me and begins to take small things out of my pockets. An elderly black man advises me to say the word "ebonic" and that it will help me avoid being robbed. At first I ignore him, but then I take his advice and it works. Next, a large crowd of angry black people surrounds me but I am afraid to antagonize them with the magical word. They take my wallet and my power tools but somehow I get them back.

Associations

Bob was a defensive and frequently argumentative patient who expressed little interest in his dreams. He offered the following associations.

> I hated college. That's when my panic attacks began. I thought I was losing my mind.

> College was a nightmare. I did poorly in school throughout high school and wanted to take a year off but my father would not permit it. That's when my panic attacks began. I could not drive and couldn't sit for my exams. I thought I was going crazy.

> I don't know anything about the black neighborhood. My family is Irish Catholic and not particularly prejudiced, although my father always told us that if we dated blacks that he would disown us. Other than that, nothing really comes to mind except that I do use power tools when I am wood-working in my shop.

Where

The dream begins with the patient back at college, where Bob's disabling panic attacks first began. It locates the dream-ego in an earlier time and place, as it attempts to return "home". This movement can be viewed as a regression but its purpose cannot be ascertained. As Freud first noted, regression can represent a non-productive movement within the psyche, or it may serve the progress of the ego.

From the psychodynamic perspective, panic attacks have been attributed to separation anxiety in individuals with insecure early attachments. Bob's mother was an alcoholic who had raised multiple young children, alone, while the patient's father worked around the clock, in order to build a highly successful business. His parents often went on lengthy vacations, leaving Bob and his siblings in the care of a series of housekeepers.

Who

At first, the dream-ego is alone but the cast of characters increases until it develops into a mob. Except for the dream-ego, all of the characters in the dream are black. Jung referred to the *shadow* (Figure 11) as the symbolic representation of psychological contents disavowed by the ego. The darkness of the "shadow" reflects the negative pole of rigid "black and white" evaluations

As Piaget noted (Reimer, Paolitto et al. 1983) rigid evaluations of good and bad are common in childhood and form the nucleus of adult morality. Cultural, religious, and family values, all contribute to the formation of *shadow*. Bob was raised in a strict Irish Catholic home and he espoused strong, and at times outrageously "politically incorrect" beliefs concerning race, religion, and the societal role of women. He proudly articulated these opinions, never considering that they might appear prejudiced and atavistic to others.

FIGURE 11   Shadow

James Barrie's *Peter Pan* (Barrie 1907), a work based on the *archetype* of the *puer aeturnus*, explores the problematic relationship between the ego and the *shadow*. In it, Peter's *shadow* has a quasi-independent life of its own. It follows Peter around but can't connect to him. In my office, I exhibit a serigraph from the Disney animation that shows Wendy attempting to sew Peter's shadow back on. For me, it is the consummate image of psychotherapy, in which much of the work represents efforts at re-integrating the *shadow*.

Two of the black characters are specified. One is a "pickpocket"; the other is an "old man". The Talmud (Taubenhaus, Wise et al. 1918) refers to two types of thieves. One uses guile in order to steal what does not belong to him, whereas the other takes things by force. Whereas the first represents no substantial threat to his victims' well-being, the other is a serious danger. The thief in the present dream has the qualities of the *Trickster*, i.e. an archetypal figure encountered in myth and folk tales. Hermes, the messenger of the Olympian Gods, was the ultimate trickster in Greek mythology. As an infant, he stole his older brother Apollo's prized cattle and then bargained with him before returning them. In the Book of Genesis, Jacob tricks his older brother Esau into selling his birthright and then steals his father's blessing. In Native American myth, animal tricksters play an important role in the creation of the world.

The *trickster* as thief "shakes up" rigid patterns within the psyche. In the dream, the thief is attempting to dismantle Bob's rigid *persona*. Bob's father had been an inveterate trickster, whose business dealings at times bordered on the illegal. A highly successful entrepreneur, he had trained his children to "bend the rules" in order to achieve their goals, while fostering intense competition between them. This predictably led to bitter conflicts, as each tried to outsmart the other, all the while vying for their father's approval. A benevolent tyrant, Bob's father watched from a comfortable distance as these internecine conflicts escalated, before firmly intervening to stop them. This continued even after his children were fully-grown, causing them to both rely upon their father and to resent his arbitrary rule. After his death, there seemed to be no limit to how vengeful the siblings could be with one another, and they eventualy were estranged from one another.

In his dealings with his family, and in general, Bob viewed him-self as a victim, disadvantaged by his perception that others did not "play fair". Yet, he was blind to his own devious behaviors. He was a strict interpreter of rules, but only when it served to frustrate the aims of his siblings and he delighted in disrupting family business deals over minor technicalities. The trickster was certainly a part of Bob's *shadow*.

The "old black man" is another aspect of *shadow*. In this dream, he is the keeper of the *noumen*, i.e., the word that carries magical powers. The ancient Indo-Europeans, whose migrations led to the widespread dissemination of language and the Aryan culture (Childe 1970), had a tripartite societal structure that included priestly, warrior, and mercantile classes. This structure is still observed in areas as diverse as ancient India and in the Celtic-derived civilizations of Europe and the British Isles. The ancient Vedic Hymns illustrate how the ancient Brahmin priests used magical words to command the activities of the Gods.

In myth, folk tales, and traditional societies, words and "names" have magical properties (Von Franz 1968). The "wise old man" (or woman) is a familiar figure in folk tales. In a typical folk-tale motif, the hero meets a *shadow* figure, e.g., a poor old man or an animal that offers the hero a magic word or phrase that he is to utter when he encounters danger. Invariably, the hero is successful only when he accepts the advice or token that has been offered, no matter how absurd it may appear at face value. In the tales of the dumbling, the sibling who is the least promising in the eyes of the father, becomes the most successful, because he is not cynically contemptuous of the advice offered by these helpful characters.

This motif symbolizes the value of engaging the *shadow*. In order to be transformative, the engagement must include an acceptance of elements that have been consciously devalued. The "wise old man" in Jungian psychology also symbolizes the *Self*, i.e., the quasi-mystical aspect of the psyche that is the source of the God-image. In the dream, the "black old man" symbolically condenses features of both *shadow* and *Self*. Bob had once held deep religious beliefs but lost his faith, after his father died. He was unable to accept his father's untimely death and like a child, he blamed God for allowing it to happen.

The dream poignantly depicts the dream-ego's mistrust and fear of the *shadow*. When the "black old man" offers the *dream-ego* a magical word that will help him, his advice is initially ignored. Predictably, this leads to greater difficulties for the *dream-ego*. Although the word "ebonic" is not found in the dictionary, its resemblance to the term "ebony" a synonym for "black" is unmistakable. Pluto, the king of the Underworld, traditionally was seated on an ebony throne, suggesting the dream's connection with the Underworld and death. The dream also appears to be implying that "black" can be used to ward off "black", following the homeopathic dictum of "like cures like". It is only by acknowledging the value of the dark side of one's personality, i.e., the *shadow*, that its threatening hold on the ego can be diminished. When the dream-ego takes the old man's advice, the thief's activities rapidly cease.

What

The dream-ego makes an error, takes the wrong train, and winds up in a "black neighborhood". Modes of transportation frequently appear in dreams and symbolize the dream-ego's relationship to the energy of the psyche. Jung and Freud differed in their conceptions of *libido*. Freud conceived of *libido* specifically as sexual energy, whereas Jung, borrowing from Eastern philosophies, conceived of *libido* broadly as the total complement of psychic energy. In his text *Symbols of Transformation*, Jung broke with Freud by suggesting that libidinal energies could be canalized along multiple pathways, with sexuality representing only one avenue of expression. In this text, I have adopted Jung's view of *libido* with respect to dream interpretation, because it allows greater flexibility.

The train symbolizes Bob's *libido*. As a passenger, the dream-ego is passive. This is a metaphor for the dream-ego being moved by the energies of the unconscious. This is in contrast to the self control that might be symbolized by the image of the dream-ego driving a car or riding a horse. The dream-ego determines that the train has taken a wrong turn. But if we adopt the view that the unconscious is correcting the one-sided perspectives of the dream-ego, then the dream-ego is being carried precisely to where it needs to go, i.e., to the land of the *shadow*.

In waking life, Bob often made "mistakes" with respect to the time and place of appointments. He reported having had difficulties in school, in part due to an inability to follow directions. He consistently attributed this to "my attention deficit disorder", implying a genetic and intractable cause of his difficulties, an indication of both his passivity and resistance to the psychotherapeutic process. Further examination revealed that his limited willingness to make efforts, particularly if he perceived that others expected something of him, belied a grandiose and entitled attitude.

As we discussed the dream, Bob found it almost impossible to fathom the idea of accepting his *shadow*, intractably persisting in his belief that only "the good" was to be embraced. This attitude was aggravated by Bob's strict Roman Catholic upbringing that posits God as the sum of all that is good (*summum bonum*) and evil as the absence of good (*privatio boni*).[1] Throughout his collected works, Jung refers to the problems that the idea of God as "all good" has caused in the Christian psyche. The rigid exclusion of "evil" from the personality contributes to the development of *shadow*.

Contrast this with the Old Testament, where God is both compassionate and vengeful. After suffering for no apparent reason, Job recognizes that there is no rational way for man to comprehend God's behavior. In *Answer to Job*, Jung examines how the God-image transforms from one of justice to one of love in the transition from Judaism to Christianity. Interestingly, in Eastern religion, the problem of good and evil does not exist *per se*. In these theosophies, God has many faces. But it is a mistake to consider the pantheon of Hindu Gods as evidence of polytheism, any more than the Christian trinity reflects polytheistic belief. Instead, it is a description of a single ineffable God with many avatars that repeatedly create, preserve, and destroy the universe.

Jung viewed confronting the *shadow* as the most pressing issue for modern man. When the *shadow* is unconscious, it is invariably projected onto others. The current world crisis, post September 11, 2001, is the result of *shadow* projections by fundamentalist Islamists and Judaeo-Christians in the West. The rhetoric of the American President that refers to "evil-doers" and "evil empires", as well as that of Islamic fundamentalists who refer to America as the "Great

Satan", are prime examples of *shadow* projections. Of course, all projections require a "hook" upon which to hang themselves, and George W. Bush and the radical Islamists have certainly provided one. When *shadow* projections between nations go unrecognized, war is too often the end result.

Crisis and Lysis

Change does not come easily, even in dreams. When a crowd of black people gathers, the *dream-ego* is reticent to use the magic word for fear of being attacked. This only increases the danger until an "ebonic" threatening mob has formed. Amplification, or what the alchemists termed *multiplicatio*, is a psychological operation evidenced in the dream by the repeated thievery and by the increasing size of the mob.

Cognitive psychologists have suggested that panic attacks may be caused by distorted interpretations of internal physical sensations, coupled to catastrophic thinking concerning their significance. When describing his panic attacks, Bob conveyed fears of losing his mind. Anxiety and catastrophic thinking are invariably the rigid dream-ego's response to its *shadow*.

Bob's relationship to his anger was dysfunctional. It surfaced either as temper tantrums or inappropriately not at all. He had adopted an unsavory habit of threatening others, particularly in his family, convinced that his overbearing stance was justified. In therapy, his anger manifested as severe passive-aggressive resistance to the use of metaphor and to interpretations. In the extreme, passive-aggressiveness is a reliable sign of serious mental illness as it betrays the underlying severity of the conflicts that inhere to autonomy and the preservation of the nuclear self. Passive-aggressive patients experience themselves as powerless and enraged. They use this unconscious mode of resistant aggression to secure the psyche from the danger of disintegration. This is likely why Bob's panic attacks were focused on fears of incipient insanity.

The dream has an interesting lysis. The mob steals the *dream-ego*'s power tools but it somehow manages to get them back. Bob initially offered no description as to how he retrieved his tools but later reported that he thought that he had done so by again uttering the word "ebonic". Power tools can symbolize *libido* and the *dream-ego's* relationship to its own power. Bob's family was constantly involved in financial squabbles, even though each member of the family was financially secure. Money was the currency of the family's struggles for power.

But despite his wealth, Bob viewed himself as powerless. He referred to himself as "the runt of the litter". He identified himself with Fredo, the ridiculed brother in the *Godfather* trilogy (Coppola, Brando et al. 1990). Like Fredo, Bob was viewed as weak and ineffective by both his parents and siblings. And like Fredo, he harbored grandiose fantasies of running the family business and was bitter when his talents were not recognized.

Having considered power as one path of libidinal canalization, the sexual implications should also be examined. Bob was uncomfortable with his body and with his sexuality. Despite being heterosexual, his homophobia was severe.

Bob was preoccupied with evoking the admiration of women and his desire to please them was rooted in oedipal dynamics. But he was unable to consider the roots of his behavior, adamantly insisting that he was independent of his variably critical and overly indulgent mother. Yet, he spent an inordinate amount of time talking about his mother in therapy, visited her frequently, persistently sought her approval, and became sullen and brooded if she appeared to be favoring another sibling.

Why

Bob brought many problems to therapy. His psychological difficulties were long-standing but they were substantially exacerbated by his father's death and by his inability to express his anger towards either of his parents directly. The *herald dream* illustrated his problems with anger and power. Bob lived in a narcissistic cocoon, immersed in grandiose fantasies, and unwilling to work. Despite little evidence to support the assertion, he repeatedly assured me that he was a genius, and perhaps he was. But he had been made effete by an overbearing father and was trapped in a negative mother complex, compulsively re-enacting a dynamic of seduction and rejection with the women he dated.

I often wondered who Bob would have been had he not been independently wealthy and mired by his father's success. Ultimately, I concluded that Bob's capacities to engage productively in the world were severely limited. He had referred to himself as a cripple and in many respects this had either been an accurate estimations of his situation or self-fulfilling prophecy. His fear of failure was profound, and his father's wealth offered a "golden parachute" so that he would not have to prove himself in the world.

As might be expected, the work in therapy was not easy. Bob was not particularly adept at working symbolically, as he was identified with the extraverted positivistic style of his father. His passive-aggression was severe and I often noted myself bristling in session. Change was slow and painful for all involved and I learned how important it was not to have any expectations of him. Bob was eventually able to recognize that he had substantial problems with disavowed anger and shame and he made modest progress in these areas. It is noteworthy that the *herald dream* ends on a positive note, suggesting that Bob may eventually reclaim his power by confronting his *shadow*.

Note

1. The radical dualism suggested by Augustine likely reflects his early membership in the gnostic Manichean movement.

CHAPTER TEN

My Big Fat Greek Wedding

A 42-year-old woman presented with concerns about her inability to make commitments in relationships. She reported the following dream in the first session. Toni was a modestly overweight but attractive and energetic woman. She had previously been in therapy but quit because "I wasn't learning anything that I didn't already know and I'm not in a position to waste money".

> I am with a friend in Greece. We are at the top of a hill descending to the sea. She is in front of me. I suggest that she leave her baggage behind but she loses her footing, falls, and the baggage pushes her down the hill towards the sea.

Associations

Toni prided herself on her keen intellect. After reporting the dream, she quickly added, "Now I guess you are going to tell me that I am moving too fast and likely to have an accident. But, she quickly added, "I didn't fall; it was my friend, not me".

Some patients instead of offering associations to their dreams rapidly reel off interpretations. But these are rarely on the mark. They are meant to short circuit inquiry and to ward off feelings of envy of the analyst, who they fear knows something they do not.

Toni used her incisive intellect as a weapon in the service of intimidating others, leaving them defensive and inclined to avoid her. Toni commented at the end of our first session that she was glad I was "smart enough to keep up with her". This signaled me that my being either too smart or not smart enough would likely cause problems in the treatment.

Where

The dream takes place on a hill in Greece. Toni was born in Greece but she had not lived there for many years. Her Greek heritage was an omnipresent feature of her narrative in therapy. She spoke of her native country with great pride but she was obviously embarrassed about her status as an immigrant with "old-world" parents who refused to acknowledge that they were no longer living in a small village.

Toni was a junior faculty member whose academic promotion had been hampered by poor interactions with her colleagues. She attributed this to the envy of her female colleagues and to being a "woman in a man's world". However, it was evident that her strong opinions and strident attitudes were generally off-putting to those around her.

Toni's major issue seemed to revolve around her competitive relationship with her mother, who did not approve of her Americanized life-style, and continually harped on the fact that Toni was not married.

The dream-ego's location "high on a hill" symbolizes its grandiosity. The loftiness depicted by the image captured Toni's tendency to engage in abstract intellectualization. Her inflation was linked to a compulsive need to establish herself as intellectually superior to others. The hill contrasts with the sea below. As we have already seen, the sea is a familiar symbol of the unconscious and of the Great Mother. The juxtaposition of the lofty heights and the sea is an imaginal expression of the archetypal *opposites* of spirit and matter.

In virtually all mythologies, except those of ancient Egypt, the sky is associated with a paternal procreative demiurge and the sea with the receptive maternal element. The Egyptians conceived of hills as the outcroppings of earth that emerged when the air howled across the primordial waters (Eliade 1963). In the first chapter of the Book of Genesis the spirit is said to hover above the waters. The Hebrew word for the primordial waters is *tehom*, cognate to the Sumerian Goddess *Tiamat* who was the feminine matrix of chaos. In the Sumerian myth (Chiera, Kramer et al. 1934), Tiamat is slain by Marduk, who cuts her into pieces, and thereby imposes *logos* onto chaos. This is a metaphor for the creation of consciousness out of the chthonic matrix of the unconscious.

Despite her ardent feminism, I wondered whether the dream-ego's position on the hill might represent Toni's identification with the masculine world. The Greek Goddess Athene was traditionally the protectress of high places. She symbolized what has been termed an "aggressive spirituality". In one version of Athene's birth, Zeus mates with the Titaness Metis and subsequently devours her while she is still pregnant with Athene.

Metis was the ancient goddess of reason and wisdom, and her daughter Athene continued this tradition after she was born directly out of Zeus' head (Figure 12). Athene is a proud female Goddess, but she is identified with the patriarchal *logos*. The dream suggests that in order for the dream-ego to access the matriarchal feminine, she will first have to descend from Athene's lofty Parthenon of ideas towards the sea.

Who

A female friend accompanies the *dream-ego*. An unidentified figure of the same sex represents a *shadow* figure or *alter ego*. An *alter ego* represents a vertical split in the ego, that yields two aspects of consciousness functioning in parallel, each unaware of each other. The fact that the figure is identified as a "friend" suggests a positive identification with the figure.

FIGURE 12   Athene

In this case, the *alter-ego* is the subject of the action of the dream, whereas the *dream-ego* stands behind her, observing, and giving advice. This was characteristic of Toni. She tended to observe others, judging their behavior, in much the same way her mother had done to her. The dream suggests that despite Toni's image of herself as a strong proactive woman, in reality, she was often weak and passive. It might further be suggested the image depicts Toni's Mother standing behind all of Toni's activities.

When

The dream takes place in the present but it is evidently linked to her earlier life in Greece. While it was plain that her Greek past continued to be the backdrop for her present life, Toni was reticent to accept that she was tied to her past.

What

The *dream-ego* warns her friend that she should divest herself of her baggage before venturing down the hill. Toni came to therapy with a large amount of "baggage". She reported problems in virtually every sector of her life, including ongoing bitter arguments with her family. Although she had previously been in treatment, she had quickly mastered the "rules" of psychotherapy, and used her intellect to defend against her shame and sadness. Joyce McDougall (McDougall 1990) has referred to the *anti-analysand* as a patient whose anxieties about sharing feelings of dependency and shame are so great that they are for all intents and purposes "incurable" through the efforts of the analyst. These patients grasp their issues intellectually, as Toni did, but they are unwilling to risk experiencing what they perceive as unbearable affects.

Toni's family history included substantial physical and verbal abuse, as well as moves to several different countries, as her father searched for gainful employment. One of Toni's central dilemmas was how to remain connected to her family and her Greek heritage without having to sacrifice her life as a professional American woman. When she made efforts to separate from her family, she was crippled by panic attacks and overwhelmed by guilt. But it was difficult for Toni to admit her continued dependency on her family and on her mother, in particular, choosing to believe instead that she was merely fulfilling her filial duty in caring for them.

The dream-ego first projects its baggage onto the *alter ego* and then advises "leaving it behind". Toni had repeatedly been advised by others to separate from her family. Instead, she continued to argue with her mother while complaining to others that she did not know what else to do. A psychoanalyst, David Shapiro (Shapiro 1981), has attributed this behavior to the hysterical style, in which productive solutions for conflicts are generally ignored, but unhesitatingly recognized when the same problems are someone else's.

Excessive splitting of the ego occurs when there has been a history of trauma. Toni's childhood had been chaotic and included both severe emotional and physical abuse. But when I suggested that she had been traumatized, Toni laughed and attributed the chaos to living in a Greek family; however, it was evident that she was aware of the truth. Whereas cultural differences must be considered when treating patients, Toni's sense of self and her ability to develop intimate relationships were severely compromised, and this cannot be attributed to cultural variation.

Crisis and Lysis

On first consideration, the dream appears to have an unsuccessful denouement. The *alter-ego* does not take the advice offered, and consequently slips, falls, and is driven down the hill by the baggage. One is reminded of the nursery rhyme of Jack and Jill tumbling down the hill while searching for "water". A slip represents a loss of one's footing. Psychoanalytically speaking, it undoes the previous stance of the ego and alters the psyche's sense of balance. It is apparently not enough for the *alter ego* to walk down the hill, instead, a change in stance and attitude is required.

Failure to take advice was a core feature of Toni's oppositional stance with others. But the dream also offered me a piece of therapeutic advice. For if I were to advise Toni to separate from her family, as her previous therapist had, she would certainly ignore me, continue to deny responsibility for her predicament, and likely prematurely terminate the treatment. Whereas, it is neither possible nor advisable for the analysts to not have a agenda, offering direct advice to patients should virtually always be avoided.

Other possible interpretations of the dream merit consideration. For example, from the perspective of self-psychology, the dream suggests a picture of Toni's narcissistic psychology, in which her self-esteem plummets under the weighty "baggage" of a harsh superego. The "true-self", symbolized by the dream-ego, protects itself by not participating in the action. The reluctance of the dream-ego to participate might also signal resistance to interpretations that might jeopardize her self-esteem. This emphasizes the role of shame in Toni's psychology and how difficult it was to penetrate her defenses without triggering unbearable shame affects.

A more optimistic perspective on the dream is that at least an aspect of the ego does eventually reach its goal, albeit in a rough and tumble manner, without relinquishing its "baggage". In fact, holding on to her past might even be necessary for Toni to one day reconcile with her split-off affects. The ability to hold all of these paradoxical interpretations, without knowing which one best applies, is an important part of therapeutic dream work.

Why

I was never completely clear as to why Toni came to see me in therapy. She remained only several months and never committed to the work. She claimed that she had mounting expenses and could not afford to continue treatment, thereby repeating her previous behavior in therapy. I was keenly aware of that eventuality and had attempted to discuss it with her beginning with the first treatment session. But in the end, I was unable to dissuade her from leaving. I am confident that Toni knew that I was aware of her issues, but the dread of experiencing her shame and the fear of separating from her family were too great. The *herald dream* confirmed that Toni had a long way to go in relinquishing her intellectual grandiosity. But it also suggested that she may reach the "sea" eventually.

CHAPTER ELEVEN

The Reptilian Brain

John was a 25-year-old man whose mother referred him to my practice concerned with his inability to engage with the world. John's own chief complaint was an ill-defined but deeply rooted fear of women. His sexual experience with women was limited and he displayed little interest in either sex. He reported feeling deeply confused about what others expected of him and what he wanted out of life.

Despite being an attractive and intelligent young man, there was something decidedly strange about John. At times, his facial expressions seemed odd and his verbal responses were frequently concrete and tangential. I wondered whether he might have a schizotypal personality, i.e., a disorder with overlap features of schizoid personality and psychosis. But, at other times, his responses were appropriate and his mannerisms unremarkable. John reported the following dream in our second session.

> I am in an office that reminds me of my father's. I see you in the next room doing "family therapy". I am holding a reptile that has wings. There is a crow in your office. It begins to transform into a dove. I am afraid that the reptile will eat the dove but instead they get along fine and fuse into one another.

Associations

John offered the following association to the dream:

> I used to go to my dad's office on the weekends. He was usually busy
> and it was boring. I like reptiles and I've had a lot of them as pets. My
> mother was scared of them and hated them.

Where

Although the dream takes place in my office, it reminded John of his
father's office that he would occasionally visit as a boy. Confusion
was a prominent feature of the dream, much as John reported it to be
in his waking life. John's father and I are both physicians, although
we practice in different fields and have never met. His mother had
suggested that John and I might work well together because his
father and I were both doctors. This was a curious conclusion, as
John reported a distant and conflicted relationship with his father.
In fact, John's association to his father's office as "boring" hinted
that he might have similar feelings about coming to see me. In fact, it
was not clear whether John had come to treatment voluntarily or at
his mother's insistence. Even after several attempts at determining
his motivations, I could not establish clarity. John's confusion had
rapidly infiltrated my countertransference.

Who

The dream cast includes the dream-ego, myself, a reptile and a bird,
i.e. a total of four characters. Numbers are significant in Jungian
dream interpretation. The number "4" has been taken to be a symbol
of wholeness, based on its traditional representation of a complete
set of elements, e.g. four seasons, four directions, four elements of
earth, wind, fire, air, and the quaternity of the Father, Son, Holy
Ghost, and an implied feminine principle.[1] The appearance of a tet-
rad in dreams, like the appearance of a circle, may be viewed as a
psychic effort towards integration.[2]

The analyst's presence in a *herald dream* reported early in the treatment suggests a strong transference response. I interpreted the fact that no actual interaction takes place between us in the dream as a transference statement concerning the emotional distance that John had experienced in relationship to his father. His fear that the reptile might devour the dove in my office was a good indicator of an early negative transference, as well as his desire to save me from his devouring oral aggression.

Reptiles were to be a repetitive element in John's dreams. For several years, he brought dreams that included lizards, snakes, and other reptiles. Reptiles are cold-blooded animals that inhabited the planet before the emergence of mammals. There is evidence that mammals are instinctively fearful of reptiles, as they were prey for larger reptilian predators. However, John was fascinated by lizards and snakes and kept them as pets. As it is not possible to develop much of a mutual relationship with a reptile, John's kinship with these creatures was in itself revealing of his fundamentally schizoid stance.

During evolution, the human brain has conserved features of the older reptilian brain. The mental features of our reptilian inheritance have been repressed with limited success by the mammalian brain.[3] Based on MacLean's model of a triune brain, psychoanalysis has conceived of certain psychological disorders, e.g. borderline personality, as reflections of inadequately inhibited primitive reptilian behavior. Like reptiles, these patients often exhibit a profound lack of trust, unbridled appetites, and diminished empathy for others.

Animals in dreams generally symbolize instinctual elements of the psyche that have not been sufficiently integrated. The crow is a large black predatory bird depicted in myth and folk-tales as a cunning animal with evil inclinations, i.e. as a theriomorphic[4] *shadow* figure. By contrast, the dove is a gentle white bird that frequently symbolizes love and peace. In Christian legend, the crow is associated with Satan, whereas the dove symbolizes the Holy Spirit that mediates the annunciation of Jesus' birth. The presence of these two birds suggests a childlike polarization of black and white; i.e. of good and bad, in John's psychology. The transition of the dream-ego's attention from me in my office to the crow and the dove is in keeping with the idea that coming to therapy had evoked primitive conflicts for John.

When

While the dream takes place in the present, it also references the office that John had visited as a child. This suggests that the past continued to influence John's present and might be re-enacted in the transference.

What

The dream begins with the dream-ego watching as I am conducting "family therapy". The image implicates the family as the proper focus of therapy. Jung believed that the cause of most childhood neurosis was to be found in the unresolved conflicts of the parents. Johns's parents had divorced when he was in his early teens and his subsequent relationship with both of his parents might best be described as troubled. Although in his mid-20's, John was naïve and childlike in many respects.

The dream-ego observes that I am conducting therapy but it does not enter the room. In many respects, John never entered therapy. Although the treatment was to last for several years, I did not got the sense that John was invested in its outcome or frankly that he had much of an idea as to how to avail himself of what was transpiring in the treatment. He would twice weekly and dutifully bring his dreams, talk about them, and then leave seemingly untouched by the experience.

The *herald dream* offered a description of John's psyche, as well as a prescription for what needed to happen in treatment. At first, the crow transforms into a dove, a metaphor for how John tended to deal with his "negative" emotions by transforming them into something "positive". It also depicts the fusion of the crow and the dove, i.e. reconciling the "good" with the "bad". Incapable of expressing his aggression directly, John adopted the false bravado that patient's with this problem often do, appearing to get angry but without passion. But he was the consummate good boy, polite, and overly compliant and watching him express his outrage was like watching a rag doll flailing about. His near complete dissociation from his sexual and aggressive drives had left John enfeebled. If

FIGURE 13   Dragon

he were to make progress, he would have to confront and integrate his *shadow*.

The winged reptile in the dream is a thinly veiled reference to a dragon (Figure 13). Dragons are mythical creatures encountered in folk tales that threaten enfeebled kingdoms powerless to defend against them.[5] Dragons demand tributes of gold or may hold a princess hostage, but as Joseph Campbell noted (Campbell 1988), since they cannot possibly have any way of enjoying gold or sex, they are actually symbols of unadulterated greed. In psychoanalysis, dragons are generally regarded as symbols of the negative feminine, symbolizing the mother who greedily holds on to her children and will not let them grow to be independent adults.

John described his mother as anxious and self-absorbed. She was an entertainer and he attributed his lack of interest in sex, in part, to feeling repulsed by her intrusive expressiveness. His ambivalence with respect to his mother was attributable to unresolved pre-oedipal and oedipal conflicts and his fear of women was rooted in an early chaotic maternal attachment. With a certain degree of upset and sadness, he reported that he dreaded approaching her for fear of being anxiously rebuffed. At the same time, his relationship to his mother was complicated by overtones of sexual seduction and by her overprotective concerns. John seemed to be virtually paralyzed by the incest taboo and by fears of reprisal by an angry oedipal father.

The dream-ego is concerned that the reptile will eat the dove in my office. This reflects John's concern that he might kill off whatever good I might have to offer him.

The oedipal triad is configured in the dream by my presence as a distant but humanized older man and by the theriomorphic dragon-as-mother. If we apply the idea that the unconscious is structured like the mother, then it is likely that John's disabling anxiety about his aggression had been transferred to him during his early inter-actions with his mother. Indeed, he reported that his mother would tend to get quite disturbed by displays of aggression and that she was generally too anxious to be a source of comfort to him as a child.

Why

John was seriously troubled when he first came to therapy. When he left several years later, he was still struggling with many problems. Although he had made substantial progress at expressing his anger, his fear of women was unresolved. The *herald dream* poignantly highlighted the major issues that John was dealing with, and offered a prescription for their solution. I worried about John's well-being while was in treatment, as well as after he left. Like so many children of divorce, he had been tragically lost in the shuffle. Now as a young adult, he was isolated and confused about how to navigate within the world.

Notes

1. Jung wrote extensively about how Christianity had dogmatically excluded the "feminine principle" and how it had insinuated it's way back into the religion via the worship of Mary. At other times, he referred to Sapientia or Sophia as the feminine element of the quaternity in the form of wisdom.
2. The etymology of the word "to heal" is controversial but has been suggested to be cognate with "wholeness".
3. MacLeans's triune brain is comprised of reptilian, paleomammalian, and neomammalian components. This model is no longer held to be accurate by most experts but it does convey the fact that the brain is an evolved organ.
4. Theriomorphic non-human creatures often represent poorly integrated archetypal instinctual features of the psyche that have not been sufficiently "humanized" by relationships with others.
5. In Chinese culture, dragons symbolize good fortune.

CHAPTER TWELVE

Out of Control

A 28-year-old female physician in training reported the next dream. She came to treatment seeking help for a long-standing eating disorder that had developed when she was in high school. When I first saw Ellen, I thought I was watching a marionette. She did not appear to be ambulating by her own effort but instead appeared to be moved along by a set of invisible strings. Her movements were jerky and tightly controlled, when she entered and left the consulting room. As she sat across from me in my office, she scrutinized my facial expressions for evidence of approval or disapproval. Ellen had been in therapy in another state and had continued to talk to her previous therapist every day on the telephone for months, until her therapist wisely insisted that she find someone else to meet with in person. Her dream was reported in the second session.

> I am in an empty auditorium. There is a grand piano in the hallway and I push it onto the stage. As I begin to play, the seats suddenly collapse on each other like dominoes and the sprinkler system turns on. There is water everywhere.

Associations

"The auditorium was in the public grade school that I attended. I don't play the piano but both my mother and brother were talented musicians."

Where

The auditorium is located in her old public school. Ellen had been a mediocre student in grade school but she excelled in high school and college, doing well enough to be accepted to medical school. Her family had been preoccupied with education and her mother had been a grade school music teacher.

When

The dream takes place in Ellen's grade school. This suggests that this was an important time with respect to her present issues. Her mother had first become ill when Ellen was nine. She suffered from a variety of poorly defined disorders that required repeated hospitalizations. Preoccupied with her illness, Ellen's mother had little time for her or for the rest of the family. These illnesses continued without remission until she died from complications of a previous surgery two years before Ellen first came to therapy. After her mother's death, Ellen was consumed by grief and anger aimed primarily at the doctors who, in her opinion, had allowed her mother to die.

Who

The dream is a solitary affair with the *dream-ego* at center stage. The image underscores her need to be the center of attention. Ellen's behavior was motivated by her need for attention and approval but she could only act when she was clear about what others expected of her.

What

At the piano recital, the dream-ego is responsible for doing everything. She must both prepare for and execute the performance with no help from others. I imagined how burdensome it would be to drag a grand piano onto a stage without assistance. But this was a fitting metaphor for Ellen's life. Her mother was a narcissistically disturbed woman who suffered from a disabling psychosomatic disorder. Her death was the result of one of multiple questionably indicated surgical procedures performed by her doctors out of desperation, in an effort to alleviate her unremitting complaints.

Ellen suffered from a chronic eating disorder and hypochondriasis. It later emerged that she had Munchausen's disease, a severe psychological illness in which patients seek out unnecessary and dangerous medical and surgical treatments for factitious disease. Early in the treatment, Ellen sheepishly admitted to having been recently hospitalized for gall bladder surgery, when she persisted in complaining of right upper quadrant pain despite a battery of tests that demonstrated no cause for her complaints. Surgery revealed a normal gall bladder without gallstones. Ellen's unnecessary surgery, like her mother's had been prompted by her unremitting complaints and the desperation of her physicians.

A piano recital should be an event of beauty and an enjoyable experience. Instead, in the dream it turns into a disaster. Pleasure was something that was not straightforward for Ellen. Her confusion, or more accurately the fusion she experienced between pleasure and pain, was clearly expressed in her waking fantasies. She sheepishly but with a glimmer of pleasure told me about a recurrent daydream in which she experienced orgasm while being surgically mutilated by a team of doctors. At the end of the fantasy, she suddenly goes into shock, and the doctors, frantically attempt to resuscitate her, but without success.

In fact, all of her medical and psychiatric treatments had been eminently unsuccessful. Ellen appeared to revel in reducing her caregivers to helplessness, paralleling her own lack of success in attempting to help her long-suffering mother. Most disturbing was the fact that this fantasy was obviously ego-syntonic for Ellen. She never complained when things turned out badly for her. And although she was not suicidal, death was always a feature of her imaginings.

As Ellen's mother had been a talented pianist, I suspected that the piano symbolized her mother—dark and heavy, but capable of exhibiting beauty, when properly "played". Ellen described sitting for hours in her mother's darkened hospital room, receiving no acknowledgment of her presence or appreciation for her efforts to visit at the end of every school day. Instead, her mother was only animated when her physicians entered the room, which was her cue to complain to them. The burden of the *dream-ego* is reminiscent of the myth of Sisyphus (Figure 14). Sisyphus betrayed Persephone the

FIGURE 14   Sisyphus and boulder

Queen of the Underworld. His punishment was to push a large boulder up a mountain, only to have it repeatedly roll back to its starting position. This mythic link between torture, masochism, and death was appropriate, as Ellen's tortured psyche was dwelling in the land of the Dead.

The futility of Sisyphus' task also illuminates what it is like to try to help a somatizing patient. Although help is sought after and initially welcomed, it is invariably rejected. The compulsion to regurgitate whatever nourishment she was offered was furthermore enacted by Ellen's bulimia. Whatever she took in from others, she willfully expelled. Ellen was skilled at playing a deadly zero-sum game.

Crisis and lysis

As soon as the recital begins, things go wrong. The empty seats fall as if pre-determined to do so. The automaticity depicted by this image is a metaphor for Ellen's drive to repeat her self-destructive behaviors. Freud examined the repetition compulsion in his 1920 monograph *Beyond the Pleasure Principle* (Freud 1920). As a result of his inability to make analytic progress with certain patients, Freud suggested that they were under the influence of a psychological death (*Thanatos*) instinct that opposed the will to live (*Eros*). He grounded this conclusion in scientific observations of other species and in his clinical experience.

Rigid repetitions are triggered by an inciting event and then play out stereotypically. It is virtually impossible to interrupt them, once they have been activated. For this reason, it is important to identify what triggers the response and to intervene before the repetition begins. The dream indicates that things go wrong when the dream-ego begins to play the piano. What might "playing the piano" symbolize? Ostensibly, one plays the piano, in order to make music. Music can evoke strong affects and emotion by virtue of its direct influence on emotion. The image of playing the piano may represent the *dream-ego's* effort at evoking an emotional response from others and at connecting with isolated affects. In addition, one "plays" the piano, a likely reference to Ellen's inability to play spontaneously.

As a child, Ellen's efforts to evoke positive responses from her mother had failed. This dysfunctional dynamic characterizes what can transpire between narcissistic mothers and their children. Any expression of Ellen's autonomy was an excuse for her mother to make her feel guilty for being ungrateful. Hypersensitive to a fault, when disappointed, Ellen's mother would reject her daughter, leaving Ellen isolated and shamed. As her mother sank increasingly into the depths of psychosomatic illness, she was no longer available to Ellen at all. Despite this, or perhaps because of it, Ellen's identification with her mother was virtually complete. By destroying herself instead of expressing her murderous hatred of her mother, as Fairbairn noted (Fairbairn 1990), she was able to preserve the all too fragile ties to a good internal object.

While her mother was still alive, Ellen spoke to her several times a day and referred to her as her "best friend". She insisted that her mother had selflessly sacrificed her life for her children. However, when questioned concerning the specifics of what her mother had done, she invariably described an anxious and depressed woman who exhibited little genuine interest in anyone but herself.

At the time that Ellen came to see me, she was in the midst of actively unraveling her career. Her psychological difficulties were profound and frankly incompatible with the effective conduct of her professional duties. But she refused to take a leave of absence from her hospital work, choosing instead to call in sick frequently, thereby disrupting the work-schedules of her colleagues. Furthermore, she inappropriately shared selected aspects of her difficulties with hospital administrators, who were not inclined to be sympathetic. Ellen refused to consider that she was irrevocably undermining her own career. As in the dream, she was acting automatically, while psychologically dissociated from her actions. By assuming an aura of naiveté, she was also able to deny her extreme degree of hateful destructiveness. But despite her obsequious style, I had the uncomfortable feeling that Ellen was capable of great "evil".

The activation of the sprinkler system that follows the calamity of the falling chairs depicts a sudden influx of water. Water is required in order to soften solid matter and to bring it into solution. In Buddhist psychology, water is considered a cohesive element that binds matter together, e.g., flour into dough, and helps to keep energy circulating. From these references it could be suggested that water was required, in order to soften the rigidity of Ellen's psyche.

Her inflexibility was exhibited in innumerable spheres from her fixed fantasies to the wooden quality of her body habitus. One is reminded of the wooden puppet Pinocchio's traveling in the belly of the whale deep within the ocean prior to his transformation into a real boy.

Water is also the stuff of tears. Despite her devotion to her mother, Ellen was unable to cry after her death. The dream image would be in keeping with the obvious need for a catharsis of grief that could free Ellen of some of her pent up emotion.

Consistent with the oedipal theme in dreams, the activation of the overhead sprinklers might also represent an impersonal father, in the form of the archetypal sky god, who sends the rains. Ellen described her father as distant and pervasively critical. After her mother's death, he quickly found a new love interest, and Ellen like the brooding Hamlet, felt betrayed by how rapidly her father had forgotten about his dead wife. Ellen's response was to construct a mental shrine to her mother, where she ritualistically honored her.

Why

This *herald dream* clearly delineated the state of Ellen's psyche and helped me to focus on the areas that required therapeutic attention. Ellen's situation was grave. She eventually revealed to me that she had been clandestinely taking a certain medication without medical indication, in order to induce a serious cardiac arrhythmia, so that she could be hospitalized and subjected to invasive tests. As is often the situation in cases of factitious disease, her physicians were at a loss as to what was causing her medical problems. Ellen's interest in psychotherapy waned as, like her mother, she increasingly began to receive the attention of "real doctors", who would attend to her serious somatic symptoms. Indeed, Ellen's mother had contemptuously dismissed the possibility that her own symptoms might be psychological in nature. Ellen's psychological identification with her mother was almost complete. The compulsive need to split psyche from soma characterizes psychosomatic illness. Its basis has been addressed by Foucault (Foucault 1954) as follows:

Illness may be perceived with an objectivity that places the ill consciousness at a maximum distance. In his effort to arrest it and to
avoid recognizing himself in it, the patient sees it as an accidental
organic process. The patient maintains his illness at the limits of his
body: omitting or denying any alteration in psychological experience,
he gives importance to, and in the end, perceives and thematizes,
only the organic contents of his experience. Far from hiding his
illness, he displays it, but only in its physiological forms. . . .

I am trained as a medical internist and continue that practice with a
particular expertise in psychosomatic disorders (Kradin 1997). To
the best of my knowledge, Ellen was not aware of my professional
interests. As I listened to Ellen in the treatment, it became increasingly evident that multiple visits to emergency rooms, psychiatric
and medical hospitalizations, and unnecessary surgeries were all
occurring outside of the consulting room. Ellen would call to tell me
that she was in one hospital or another recovering from an operation, or receiving electroconvulsive therapy for a severe depression
that she did not have. As expected, none of these interventions were
effective.

I looked on at a distance and in horror as these events unfolded,
aware of what was occurring but effectively helpless to intervene without destroying the analysis. Ellen's other caretakers were
unaware of the full range of what was transpiring, as she was
successful in splitting her care, a reflection of her own intrapsychic
compartmentalization. I have written elsewhere, that in my opinion
one of the grave errors in the treatment of psychosomatic disorders
is the team approach, in which different care providers provide different perspectives, all too often without sufficient integration,
thereby increasing the excessive tendency of these patients to split
internal and external objects, as well as psyche and soma (Kradin
1997). When, at Ellen's insistence, I was compelled to discuss her
case with her other care providers, I was unable to convince them
that their efforts to intervene with short-term approaches, surgeries,
and medications, were all doomed to fail. There can be no quick fix
for psychosomatic disorders of this magnitude. Instead, Ellen's need
to be seen and heard, as evidenced by the dream recital, would
require long-term psychotherapy, and consolidation of her care, if
she were to come to grips with the grief and rage that were fueling
her repetitive self-destructive behaviors.

Unfortunately, despite the desperate efforts by a host of well-intentioned physicians to stabilize her situation, Ellen eventually required long-term psychiatric hospitalization and she was forced to resign her duties as a physician. In all honestly, I was frankly relieved that she would no longer be caring for the sick, as she was the one who desperately needed help. Unfortunately, due to the progressive dissolution of the therapeutic boundaries and the increasing focus on medical and pharmacological interventions, it ultimately was impossible for me to continue working with her. I count this as one of the most frustrating cases in my career. Ellen had defeated all of us, but it was she who had been lost.

CHAPTER THIRTEEN

Dreams in Supervision

Working with *herald dreams* in supervision can be a rewarding educational experience. Working in group supervision tends to yield a greater number of potentially illuminating associations. There is a certain infectious enthusiasm that tends to enhance the joy and excitement of working with symbolic material. There is also less concern about being criticized than in one on one supervision, so that the spontaneity of responses is enhanced.

A trainee in a supervision group reported the following *herald dream* of a 42-year-old woman who she had been treating in therapy for several months.

> I am going to visit my mother. She is in a nursing home. It is a stormy night and I am afraid. Two girls accompany me. I run to a cemetery. There is a mausoleum there. I lie in a coffin and feel safe.

When I supervise dream work, I generally ask not to be told anything about the patient at first. This allows me to convey directly to the group that there is an objective aspect to dreams that allows one to intuit accurate information concerning the dreamer without associations or knowledge of the developmental history. After the group has formulated a first impression of the dream, I invite the supervisee to tell us about the dreamer as well as the dreamer's associations. At that point, the initial "hypotheses" are modified appropriately.

Associations

"My mother used to work in a nursing home."

New trainees welcome bits of information like this, as they conclude that they have been given an important piece of the dream puzzle for free. So they are often initially dismayed when I advise them to ignore "the facts" and to concentrate exclusively on the dream's symbolic implications. This approach invariably has its rewards, as most trainees tend to err early in their career on the side of what is concrete versus metaphoric. In order to accomplish this goal, I ask the group to entertain all of their possible associations to the specific images of the dream, until their ideas have been exhausted. In this case, I asked "what comes to mind when you consider a nursing home?" The group associated to old age, illness, dependency, depression, breast-feeding, and nurses. As they amplify the image, the group generally becomes more willing to take chances, so that increasingly, new possibilities begin to emerge.

I next asked the group to consider what it might mean symbolically to have a "mother" in a "nursing home"? Now instead of the straightforward answer that "mother used to work there", the group considered the symbolic possibilities. Was the dreamer's mother physically or mentally ill? Was she dependent on the care of others? What role did nursing play in the mothering that the dreamer received?

The symbolic approach was next applied to questions that might have specific importance for the dreamer. What does it mean that the dream-ego "has gone to visit her mother"? Does this represent a desire to be psychologically closer, i.e. identified with her? If this is true, then the group's associations to the mother might also be expected to hold true for the dreamer?

The dream now shifts to the image of a storm. Having previously considered the archetype of the patriarchal sky God (Figure 15), might this image symbolize an impersonal and "stormy" father? How may a "storm" refer to the dreamer's affect? Are we perhaps examining the dream of a woman with "affective storms", like those associated with bipolar disease or borderline personality?

It is evident that the storm frightens the dream-ego and it is at that point that two girls appear. Are these *shadow* figures representing multiple splits in the dream-ego? In mythology, dual figures represent the guardians of the threshold and they were often seen outside of ancient temples, guarding their contents but also helping to delineate what was sacred from profane.[1] As these figures appear to arise with the storm and the dream-ego's fear, are they meant to "guard" the dream-ego in its response to a severe psychic trauma by protecting it from the contents of the unconscious?

FIGURE 15   Zeus and thunderbolt

Finally the *dream-ego* enters a cemetery. A cemetery is a place where the dead are laid to rest. How does death figure in the dreamer's psychology? We have already encountered the nursing home with its morbid implications and now we are presented with a cemetery. Might this patient be morbidly depressed or physically ill? As dreams invariably precede changes within consciousness could this image augur a serious depression or illness?

The dream-ego's response to trauma is to lie still in a coffin. The possible behavioral responses to danger include fighting, fleeing, or freezing. I interpreted the dream-ego's placement in the coffin as an imitation of death, enacted via the freezing defense, the latter adopted when neither fighting nor fleeing are possible, as is often true of early sexual trauma. This image of death within life is a metaphor of psychological dissociation and the post-traumatic depression that follows sexual trauma. The association of death and sexual trauma is seen in the myth of Demeter and Persephone, where the forceful abduction and rape of Persephone by Hades, takes her to the Land of the Dead.

As previously noted, I generally look for the oedipal implications of dreams. If mother is in a "nursing home" and the father is represented by a "storm" what might that imply? Finally, what are the transference implications of the dream? Is the therapist the "mother in the nursing home" or the "dreaded storm?" Is there fear related to this stage of the treatment?

Together we arrived at the following interpretive hypothesis. The dreamer is psychologically identified with her mother who she sees as frail and dependent. The "return" is a regression of the ego and could indicate an immanent depression. This view of the mother contrasts with the image of the impersonal threatening father. The stormy father and the weak dependent mother, coupled with the fear of the storm, suggest trauma and a possible incest history. The presence of the two supportive isosexual figures, consistent with the splitting of the ego, defends the central ego from elements repressed within the unconscious, supports the posited history of trauma.

From the transference perspective, the group decided that the therapist should consider whether she might also be seen by the patient, as the frail mother who could not protect her from trauma and whether there is unconscious anger in the treatment that was not being recognized.

We learned from the supervisee that the dreamer was a middle-aged woman with a history of paternal sexual abuse that had continued for many years. Her father was an alcoholic and prone to rages when drunk. Her mother was indeed described as weak and dependent and unable to help stop the abuse.

It also became evident that the supervisee had missed several sessions because of an illness in her own family and that the patient had been able for the first time to express her dissatisfaction about the therapist's absence. Within two weeks of reporting the dream, the patient required hospitalization for a major depression.

The approach to the *herald dream* yielded a highly accurate assessment of the patient's core issues, in the absence of her personal associations. As a result of the dream analysis, the supervisee was able to recognize the continued importance of trauma in her patient's history and to consider the possible ways in which her patient might express herself in the transference.

Note

1. These were often located outside of temples and are still used in the design of buildings, e.g. the formidable stone lions that stand outside the entrance to the New York Public Library.

CHAPTER FOURTEEN

Conclusion

T he psyche is a symbolic organ whose referents span the spectrum from the personal to the collective. As it is not possible to penetrate a symbol fully, one can only intuit its implications. The idea of circumambulating a symbol captures the sense of what it means to look at a symbol from all possible directions, and then to look at it yet again. The limits of dream interpretation are imposed by the personal experience of the dreamer, whereas archetypal referents expand the dreamer's collective awareness. In practice, I aim my interpretations at the intersection of these two domains, what I term the *zone of individuation.*

There is no single meaning that can or should be ascribed to a dream. Instead there is always a set of potential meanings, some of which will "feel" correct in the context of the treatment. Jung used to say that a dream interpretation was right if it evoked an "ah-ha" response from the dreamer. But in the final analysis, interpretations are largely based on their aesthetic appeal. Theoretical physicists and mathematicians rely on their skills, intuitions, experience, and sense of symmetry in determining whether a theorem should be accepted or rejected. In many respects, the same is true of dream interpretation.

In practice, I will work with the dreamer to generate several interpretations. I will attempt to interpret the dream from both its subjective and objective perspectives and make note of both the personal and *archetypal* implications of the dream. With patients who have limited educational background and who may be sensitive about what they do not know, and with those who demand unwavering attention to their personal issues, I will choose not to share the *archetypal* perspectives but will use them to guide my own thoughts about the dreamer.

It is always important to listen for the possible transference implications of the dream. It should be taken as a truism that the dream is in part directed at the analyst, so that references to what may be occurring unconsciously for the patient and with respect to the treatment should not go unrecognized. Whereas it may appear difficult to consider all of these elements at once, with practice it becomes relatively easy to do.

The Oedipal myth is a dominant theme in treatment because it addresses the invariable triadic nature of the family. I can virtually always find reference to it in a dream. However, from the Jungian perspective it is only one of the dream's many possible mythical referents. Jung recognized that most of us are living versions of myths that have been explicated by the ancients. Some of us are heroes like Ulysses, narcissistically vulnerable like Achilles, women who resemble Demeter, Athene or Artemis, and it is possible that we are all, Oedipus or Electra, as well.

Many on either side of the Freud/Jung divide argue that their approaches are mutually exclusive. This is not my impression. I am not an ideologue and it is doubtful that the field is well served by rigid ideas of any sort. The schools of depth psychology have already suffered severely by virtue of their reticence to admit new ideas.

I do not agree with Freud's approach to dream interpretation but I do find great merit in his concepts of transference, repetition compulsion, and the defenses of the ego. At the same time, with Jung, I believe that the unconscious is the source of our creativity and that the dream is its most excellent and wondrous manifestation. And although I do not primarily emphasize the religious aspects of the psyche in my practice, it is impossible for me to reduce them, as Freud did, to the level of personal illusion. Freud gave us a theory in the service of specifics, whereas Jung's theory was predominantly in service of transcendence. Both are required, if the full spectrum of the activities of the human psyche is to be appreciated.

In my opinion, one cannot practice depth psychology optimally without working with dreams. I have had many patients who dream infrequently. Knowing that the unconscious is always operating in the room, I have no difficulty conducting a treatment without dreams. But it is my definite impression that progress in such cases is slower than when there is regular dreamwork. Dreamwork is not merely an exercise; it is an important therapeutic approach. It is also an effective way of knowing where things stand when the verbal discourse of therapy feels like it has entered the doldrums.

I can think of no more exciting or therapeutic approach than working with dreams in depth. It is my hope that the reader will have gleaned sufficient confidence from considering the examples in this text to embark on their own systematic approach to dream interpretation, regardless of their training and therapeutic orientation.

REFERENCES

American Psychiatric Association (1994). *Diagnostic Criteria from DSM-IV*. Washington, DC: The Association.

Aristotle (1985). *The Collected Works of Aristotle*. New York: Random House.

Barrie, J. M. (1907). *Peter Pan in Kensington Gardens*. London: Hodder & Stoughton.

Black, E., & J. G. Neihardt (1932). "Black Elk speaks being the life story of a holy man of the Ogalala Sioux", as told to John G. Neihardt (Flaming Rainbow). New York Rahway, NJ: William Morrow & Company; printed in the USA by Quinn & Boden Company, Inc.

Campbell, J. (1949). *The Hero with a Thousand Faces*. New York: Pantheon Books.

Campbell, J. (1988). *Power of Myth*. New York: First Anchor Books.

Campbell, J., & M. J. Abadie (1974). *The Mythic Image*. Princeton, NJ: Princeton University Press.

Cantor, N. F., Aristotle, *et al.* (1968). *Ancient Thought: Plato and Aristotle*. Waltham, MA: Blaisdell Publishing Co.

Chiera, E., S. N. Kramer, *et al.* (1934). *Sumerian Epics and Myths*. Chicago, IL: The University of Chicago Press.

Childe, V. G. (1970). *The Aryans: A Study of Indo-European Origins*. Port Washington, NY: Kennikat Press.

Coppola, F. F., M. Brando, *et al.* (1990). "The Godfather". Hollywood, CA: Paramount Home Video.

146

Crick, F., & G. Mitchison (1983). The function of dream sleep. *Nature* 304: 111–114.

Damasio, A. R. (2000). *The Feeling of What Happens: Body and Emotion in the Making of Consciousness*. New York: Harcourt Inc.

Edelman, G. (1989). *The Remembered Present*. New York: Basic Books.

Edinger, E. F. (1972). *Ego and Archetype: Individuation and the Religious Function of the Psyche*. New York: Putnam.

Einstein, A., & Readex Microprint Corporation (1960). *Collected Writings (1901–1956)*. New York: Readex Microprint Corp.

Eliade, M. (1963). *Patterns in Comparative Religion*. New York: New American Library.

Ellenberger, H. F. (1970). *Discovery of the Unconscious: The History and Evolution of Dynamic Psychiatry*. New York: Basic Books.

Erikson, E. (1950). *Identity and the Life Cycle*. Boston, MA: Harvard University Press.

Fairbairn, W. (1990). *Psychoanalytic Studies of the Personality*. New York: Routledge.

Foucault, M. (1954). *Mental Illness and Psychology*. Berkeley: University of California Press.

Foucault, M. (1994). *The Birth of the Clinic*. New York: Vintage.

Fraser, J. T. (1975). *Of Time, Passion, and Knowledge*. Princeton, NJ: Princeton University Press.

Freud, S. (1900). *The Interpretation of Dreams*. London: The Hogarth Press.

Freud, S., Ed. (1900). *The Interpretation of Dreams: Collected Works of Sigmund Freud*, Vol XIX. London: Hogarth.

Freud, S. (1901). "On Dreams". *S.E.* 5: 631–714.

Freud, S. (ed.) (1914). On narcisssism: An introduction, in J. Strachey, *The Standard Edition of the Collected Works of Sigmund Freud*. London: Hogarth Press.

Freud, S. (1920). Beyond the pleasure principle, in J. Strachey, *The Standard Edition of the Collected Works of Sigmund Freud*. London: Hogarth Press.

Freud, S. (1923). The Ego and the Id, in J. Strachey, *The Standard Edition of the Collected Works of Sigmund Freud*. London: Hogarth Press.

Fromm, E. (1941). *Escape from Freedom*. New York: Rinehart.

Frye, N. (1982). *The Great Code*. New York: Harcourt.

Graves, R. (1924). *The Meaning of Dreams*. London: Cecil Palmer.

Graves, R. (1988). *The Greek Myths*. Mount Kisco, NY: Moyer Bell.

Greenberg, J. R. (1991). *Oedipus and Beyond: A Clinical Theory*. Cambridge, MA: Harvard University Press.

Harris, I. D. (1962). Dreams about the analyst. *International Journal of Psychoanalysis* 43: 151–158.

Hillman, J. (1975). *The Dream and the Underworld*. New York: Harper & Row.

Hillman, J. (1976). *Re-visioning Psychology*. New York: HarperCollins.

Hobson, J., & R. McCarley (1977). The brain as a dreamstate generator: An activation synthesis hypothesis of the dream process. *American Journal of Psychiatry* 134: 1345–1348.

James, W. (1890). *Principles of Psychology*. New York: Henry Holt and Co.

Jamison, K. (1993). *Touched with Fire*. New York: Free Press.

Jouvet, M. (1999). *The Paradox of Sleep*. Boston, MA: MIT Press.

Jung, C. (1946). On the nature of the psyche in the structure and dynamics of the psyche, in H. Read, M. Fordham, G. Adler and W. McGuire *The Collected Works of C. G. Jung*, Vol. 8. Princeton, NJ: Princeton University Press.

Jung, C. (1946). The psychology of the transference in the practice of psychotherapy, in H. Read, M. Fordham, G. Adler and W. McGuire *The Collected Works of C. G. Jung*, Vol 16. Princeton, NH: Princeton University Press.

Jung, C. (1952). On the nature of dreams in the structure and dynamics of the psyche, in H. Read, M. Fordham, G. Adler and W. McGuire *The Collected Works of C. G. Jung*, Vol. 8. Princeton, NJ: Princeton University Press.

Kagan, J. (2002). *Surprise, Uncertainty, and Mental Structures*. Cambridge, MA: Harvard University Press.

Kant, I. (1781). *Critique of Pure Reason*. London: Longmans, Green & Co.

Kernberg, O. F. (1997). *Borderline Conditions and Pathological Narcissism*. Northvale, NJ: J. Aronson.

Kerr, J. (1992). *A Dangerous Method*. New York: Vintage.

Khan, M. M. (1976). The changing use of dreams in psychoanalytic practice. In search of the dreaming experience. *International Journal of Psychoanalysis* 57(3): 325–330.

Klein, M. (1984). *The Collected Writings of Melanie Klein*. New York: MacMillan.

Kohut, H. (1971). *The Analysis of the Self: A Systematic Approach to the Psychoanalytic Treatment of Narcissistic Personality Disorders*. New York: International Universities Press.

Kohut, H. (1984). *How Does Analysis Cure?* Chicago, IL: University of Chicago Press.

Kradin, R. (1997). The psychosomatic symptom and the self: A siren's song *Journal of Analytical Psychology* 42: 405–423.

Kradin, R. (2004) The placebo response complex. *Journal of Analytical Psychology* 49: 617–634.

Laozi, J. Ramsay, *et al.* (1993). *Tao Te Ching: A New Translation*. Rockport, MA: Element.

Lewis, H. B. (1959). Organization of the self as reflected in manifest dreams. *Psychoanalysis Review* 46: 21–35.

McDougall, J. (1990). *Theaters of the Mind*. New York: Norton.

Mèuller, F. M. (1879). *The Upanishads*. Oxford: The Clarendon Press.

Mitchell, S. (2000). *Bhagavad Gita: A New Translation*. New York: Harmony Books.

Otto, R. (1923). *Idea of the Holy*. London: Oxford University Press.

Pinker, S. (2002). *The Blank Slate: The Modern Denial of Human Nature*. New York: Viking.

Rabaté, J.-M. (2003). *The Cambridge Companion to Lacan*. Cambridge, MA: Cambridge University Press.

Reimer, J., D. P. Paolitto, *et al.* (1983). *Promoting Moral Growth: From Piaget to Kohlberg*. New York: Longman.

Samuels, A. (1985). *Jung and the Post-Jungians*. London/New York: Tavistock/Routledge.

Schore, A. N. (1994). *Affect Regulation and the Origin of the Self*. New Jersey: Lawrence Erlbaum Associates.

Schwartz-Salant, N. (1982). *Narcissism and Character Transformation: The Psychology of Narcissistic Character Disorders*. Toronto, Canada: Inner City Books.

Shapiro, D. (1981). *Autonomy and Rigid Character*. New York: Basic Books.

Sonenberg, J. (2004). *Dreamwork for Actors*. New York: Routledge.

Sontag, Susan (2004) *Regarding the Pain of Others*. New York: Picador.

Sulloway, F. (1992). *Freud: Biologist of the Mind*. Cambridge, MA: Harvard University Press.

Symington, Neville (1993) *Narcissism: A New Theory*. London: Karnac.

Taubenhaus, G., I. M. Wise, *et al.* (1918). *New Edition of the Babylonian Talmud*. Boston, MA: The Talmud society.

Tyndale, W., & J. Rogers (1549). *The Byble*. London: Thomas Raynalde and William Hyll.

Van de Castle, R. (1994). *Our Dreaming Mind*. New York: Random House.

Veith, I. (1965). *Hysteria: History of a Disease*. Chicago, IL: University of Chicago Press.

Von Franz, M.-L. (1991). *Dreams*. Boston, MA: Shambhala.

Von Franz, M.-L. (1968). *Interpretation of Fairy Tales*. Chicago, IL: Northwestern University Press.

Winnicott, D. W. (1965). *The Maturational Processes and the Facilitating Environment*. London: Hogarth.

INDEX